1 Introduction

From shopping to telecommuting, the Internet has altered how, when and where individuals conduct a remarkable array of activities. Residential high speed Internet subscriptions have grown at a pace that reflects its widespread usefulness: between 2000 and 2009 usage rates rose from 5 percent to 74 percent, a change which few technologies in recent history can match for speed and depth of diffusion.[1] Yet, scant evidence has been brought to bear upon the question of whether or not this technology has altered individual labor market outcomes.[2] This is particularly striking given economists have recognized the potential for the Internet to change labor markets for some time (e.g., Autor, 2001). This paper provides new evidence on the impact of Internet technology in the labor market and finds that home, high speed Internet has increased married women's labor force participation.

The potential effects of Internet usage on labor supply are multi-dimensional because of the many different ways the Internet is used. Home Internet can reduce the time and monetary costs of working by allowing individuals to work from home, and it can reduce search frictions in the labor market by connecting potential employees to employers. It can also save users time in home production tasks like shopping and paying bills, freeing up time to engage in market work. But the Internet offers users a wide range of new entertainment options, which may mitigate any positive effects. The net effect of home Internet use on labor supply depends on the extent to which individuals use Internet for each of these activities and the responsiveness of individual labor supply along each margin.

One reason for the scarcity of empirical work on Internet usage is the inherent difficulty in establishing a causal relationship between Internet usage and individual outcomes: Internet users are not randomly assigned and take up is likely to be endogenous to labor market

---

[1] Usage rates were calculated from Current Population Survey data. Faulhaber (2002, figure 10-1) compares broadband diffusion to VCR and wireless phone diffusion. Greenwood et al. (2005, figure 1) displays trends in appliance diffusion. Of the technologies examined by those authors, only microwave ovens diffused at close to a similar pace (3 percent to 60 percent from 1975 to 1986).

[2] The exception is the more focused literature on Internet job search (e.g., Kuhn and Skuterad, 2004; Stevenson, 2009; Kroft and Pope, 2010; Kuhn and Mansour, 2011; Brencic, 2012).

outcomes. To overcome this potential bias, I propose an instrumental variables (IV) strategy which exploits cross-state variation in supply-side constraints to high-speed Internet access. Unlike dial-up Internet, high-speed Internet installation required substantial investments by Internet service providers and access was neither immediate nor uniformly distributed across locations. From an Internet service provider's perspective, multiple family dwellings were easier and more profitable for installation. Motivated by this differential investment incentive, I show that geographic variation in the housing infrastructure –namely, the percent of the state population residing in a multiple family dwelling– can predict trends in Internet access and usage. Conditional on state and year fixed effects, and a host of time-variant state-level labor and housing market indicators, the identification assumption is that the fraction of a state residing in multiple family dwellings would not have been correlated with subsequent trends in labor supply in the absence of broadband Internet diffusion. A placebo test indicates that the instrument cannot predict trends in labor supply prior to the diffusion of high-speed Internet.

To estimate the effect of Internet usage and labor supply I employ micro-level Current Population Survey (CPS) data on self-reported home high speed Internet usage and labor market outcomes. Using the proposed instrumental variables strategy, I find Internet usage leads to an an 18.6 percentage point increase in married women's labor force participation. These effects are substantially larger than the OLS estimate, but a key difference between the OLS and linear IV estimates is the IV estimates apply only to marginal Internet adopters (Imbens and Angrist, 1994). If there is heterogeneity in treatment effects, so that women who are induced into Internet usage by the instrument are women who can benefit more from its usage, the IV estimate may overstate the overall causal effect.

To explore whether the IV estimates are representative of the population at large I estimate marginal treatment effects (MTEs), which describe how the effects of Internet usage vary as different types of women are induced into Internet usage at different values of the instrument. Although somewhat imprecisely estimated, the shape of the distribution of MTEs is indicative of significant heterogeneity in the effects of Internet usage across the population of married women. Moreover, an examination of the weights that the linear IV estimator places on each part of the distribution of MTEs provides evidence of positive selection bias in the IV estimate. I then re-weight the MTEs using population weights to estimate an average effect that does not suffer from this selection bias and find that high speed Internet usage leads to an average 6.7 percentage point increase in participation. Finally, I look at the average demographic characteristics of women with positive treatment effects. I find that large, positive effects on labor supply are strongly associated with having a college education and, to a lesser extent having children (particularly school-aged children).

The main scholarly contribution of this paper is to provide an empirical examination of how high-speed home Internet technology has affected labor market outcomes. This adds to a more focused literature that has considered the use of Internet technology as a tool for job search (Kuhn and Skuterad, 2004; Stevenson, 2009; Kuhn and Mansour, 2011; Kroft and Pope, 2010; Brencic, 2012). Further, this work contributes to the development of a broad understanding of how technological progress in the home affects economic outcomes. Similar to work by Greenwood, Sheshadri, and Yorukoglu (2005), who study the diffusion of washing machines, microwaves, and other home technologies, I find a substantial impact of a home-based technology on female labor force participation.

The finding that Internet technology is important for the labor supply decisions of highly educated women with families suggests high-speed Internet facilitates work-family balance. The conflicting demands of work and family are often thought to be responsible for the persistence of the gender wage gap and the relative lack of women in leadership roles (e.g., Bertrand and Hallock, 2001; Sasser, 2005; Black, Haviland, Sanders, and Taylor, 2008; Bertrand, Goldin, and Katz, 2009). This paper contributes to an empirical literature which has shown that family-friendly workplace policies can improve the labor market outcomes of women with families (Ruhm, 2004; Baker and Milligan, 2008; Herr and Wolfram, 2009). Furthermore, I find suggestive evidence that this technology has allowed women to increase their labor supply via telework. This speaks to the potential for telework and flexible scheduling policy to encourage labor market entry.

The results indicate that high speed Internet has the largest, positive impact on the labor supply decisions of women with a college education and children. This reconciles well with aggregate trends in labor supply over the period studied. Figure 1 displays trends in labor force participation for married women from 1980 to 2010 from the Current Population Survey, shown separately by level of education and the presence of children. After almost of century of secular increases in married women's labor supply, growth stalled and participation rates fell in the mid-1990s. This decline in participation (particularly among highly educated women) garnered significant attention in the media and popularized the term "opting out"; a hypothesis that highly educated women were choosing motherhood over their careers (Belkin, 2003; Wallis, 2004; Story, 2005).[3] Figure 1 displays another noteworthy trend that has garnered less attention: starting in the early 2000s, labor force participation began to rise among highly educated women with children. My results suggest that high speed Internet usage can help to explain this differential increase.[4]

Average rates of Internet usage mask large disparities in usage by level of education: while 80 percent of college graduates had home high speed Internet subscriptions in 2009, only 30 percent of high school dropouts had subscriptions.[5] This gap in usage has been called a "digital divide," and is often attributed cost prohibitions or lack of availability in poor neighborhoods. Yet, among individuals who do not use high speed Internet, the most commonly cited reason for non-use is lack of interest, not price or lack of access (Smith, 2010).[6] This is indicative that inequality in the economic benefits of usage –not access– has

---

[3] Empirical evidence on the topic has been mixed (Boushey, 2005; Herr and Wolfram, 2009; Macunovich, 2010). As evidenced in figure 1, the decline in labor force participation in the mid 1990s was not limited to college educated women with children, but also less educated women with children and college educated women without children.

[4] Note that this group's employment rates (conditional on participation) fell during the 2007-2009 recession, as they did for most other demographic groups.

[5] Author's calculation from CPS.

[6] 48 percent of non-users report lack interest/relevance as the main reason for not using high speed Internet. 21 percent report price and 6 percent report availability as the main reason for not using the Internet (Smith, 2010).

led to unequal rates of take-up across groups. I find empirical support for heterogeneity in the benefits of home broadband usage in the labor market. Thus, this paper speaks to potential for various policy levers to increase usage of Internet services, and for whom increased access is likely to be important.

2 Conceptual Framework

There is a large literature in neo-classical economics that attempts to understand the determinants of individual labor supply decisions. In the simplest, static, consumer choice framework an individual faces a trade-off between consumption and leisure, and allocates time between the home and the market in order to maximize current period welfare. Becker (1965) introduced the notion that time spent at home is not only spent in leisure, but is also used productively to produce commodities like meals or clean laundry. Commodities are produced using various combinations of time and market purchased inputs, and individuals face a trade-off not only between consumption of different commodities, but also between using time or purchased inputs in production. For example, one faces a choice between watching television and cleaning their home, as well as between ordering take-out and preparing a meal from scratch. Labor supply decisions depend upon a comparison between the value of time spent engaged in market work (the wage) and the value of time spent at home (the reservation wage), where the reservation wage is a function of preferences over commodities and the substitutability of time and inputs in production.

Home Internet is used for a wide range of activities, many of which could plausibly affect the wage or reservation wage. Figure 2 displays trend data on Internet usage for different activities, calculated from the PEW Internet and American Life Survey for 2000-2010.[7] Figure 2(a) displays Internet usage for each activity "within the past year", while

---

[7]PEW Internet and American Life Project "Usage Over Time" data can be found online at http://pewinternet.org/Static-Pages/Trend-Data-(Adults)/Usage-Over-Time.aspx. The PEW Internet and American Life Project bears no responsibility for the interpretations presented or conclusions reached in this paper.

figure 2(b) displays Internet usage for each activity "yesterday." The data indicates that individuals use the Internet for a wide range of activities at high rates, including tasks like shopping, banking, work, and job search, as well as "just for fun." Moreover, intensity of usage for most activities has increased over time, as indicated by increasing rates of usage "yesterday." This provides prima facie evidence that the effects of Internet usage are likely to be multidimensional.

One channel via which home Internet might affect labor supply is through it's usage in leisure and home production activities. In this case, home Internet represents a technological advance in inputs to production. For home produced goods like shopping or paying bills, a technological improvement will tend to reduce the time agents need to spend in those tasks, reducing the reservation wage and increasing participation for those who are on the margin. This is because the elasticity of substitution between time and inputs in production is relatively high for home production goods, so an individual will tend to substitute the new technology for their own time. (Aguiar and Hurst, 2007). For example, although goods and services purchased online are nearly identical to those purchased offline, purchases online tend to require a smaller time investment than those offline. For leisure goods, the elasticity of substitution between time and inputs tends to be smaller, and it is more difficult to substitute technology for time to produce identical goods. For example, watching a movie or playing a game requires a similar time investment whether it's done online or offline. If Internet technology enhances leisure activities so that they are more enjoyable than their offline counterparts, individuals will want to substitute towards time spent in leisure, leading to an increase in the reservation wage and a decline in participation for those who are on the margin.

Home Internet may also alter labor supply decisions by allowing individuals to engage in telework (conducting some or all hours of market work remotely). Telework can increase the wage by reducing commute times (and hence, lost wages). Recent work by Black, Kolesnikova, and Taylor (2008) finds some support for this hypothesis by providing evidence that female labor force participation rates are lower in places with longer commute times. Telework might also increase wages by enhancing productivity through reductions in absenteeism and workplace distractions, and recent work by Bloom et al. (2012) provides experimental evidence that telework can improve worker productivity. Telework opportunities could also alter the reservation wage by reducing pecuniary and non-pecuniary costs to working, such as child care expenses or psychic costs of being away from children while at work.

The most well studied interaction between the Internet and labor markets is Internet job search, although empirical evidence has been somewhat mixed on the effectiveness of Internet as a tool for job search. Kuhn and Skuterad (2004) study the effect of Internet search on unemployment durations using data from the CPS and find that Internet search increases unemployment durations. Subsequent work, however, has tended to find the opposite result (Stevenson, 2009, Kuhn and Mansour, 2011) or no relationship (Kroft and Pope, 2010). These studies have all focused on unemployment durations as the outcome, but Internet search could also theoretically affect participation decisions by allowing individuals to observe higher wage or better matched jobs, effectively raising the market wage.

In sum, the variety of uses of Internet technology lead to an ambiguous prediction for the overall net effect of Internet usage on labor supply, which will depend upon (1) the extent to which individuals use Internet for work, job search, home production and leisure and (2) the responsiveness of individual labor supply along each margin. The sign and magnitude of the net effect will ultimately be an empirical question.

3 Empirical Framework

3.1 Data

The primary data source for this paper is the Current Population Survey (CPS). The CPS is a monthly survey which collects information on labor market outcomes and demographic characteristics of its participants. In addition to the main labor force and demographic information, the CPS collects additional supplemental information on its participants which varies from month to month. The surveys I employ are the months in which information on Internet usage was collected: the August 2000 and September 2001 Computer and Internet Use Supplement, and the October 2003, 2007, and 2009 School Enrollment supplements.[8] The CPS is uniquely suited for this study because it is contains extensive information on individual's current labor supply, demographic characteristics, and current Internet usage for the period of time in which high speed Internet diffused. Table 1 summarizes the CPS data.

3.2 Background on Broadband Internet Diffusion

High speed, or broadband Internet became available to residential consumers in the late 1990s and early 2000s. The alternative to high-speed broadband Internet is dial-up Internet, which was first offered to residential customers in 1995 after the privatization of the Internet. Dial-up uses the existing phone line and does not require any installation from the Internet service provider (ISP), so access was essentially universal and adoption was driven purely by consumer demand. Although most businesses invested in high-speed broadband Internet in the mid 1990s, the service was not offered to residential customers until the end of the decade. The term "broadband" refers to "advanced communications systems capable of providing high-speed transmission of services such as data, voice, and video over the Internet and other networks" (F.C.C., 2010). Transmission can be provided by a wide range of technologies, including digital subscriber lines (DSL), fiber optic cable, coaxial cable, wireless technology, and satellite (F.C.C., 2010). For the majority of residential consumers, the ISP was an existing cable company transmitting through a combination of coaxial and fiber optic cable, or an existing phone company transmitting through DSL.

---

[8]Information on Internet usage was also collected in the 1997 and 1998 Internet Supplements. I do not use those years because it is not possible to separately identify high-speed from dial-up internet users in those years.

Broadband access was (and still is) not universal. Cable and phone companies had to retrofit existing lines to enable high-speed two-way traffic. For cable companies, this included laying new fiber-optic lines and installing expensive operating switches and servers (Faulhaber, 2002; Greenstein and Prince, 2007). DSL from phone companies used existing phone lines, but in some areas existing wiring was not of sufficient quality and needed to be upgraded. Moreover, the phone companies were not generally aware of which areas would need upgraded until they arrived for installation (Grubesic and Murray, 2002; Faulhaber, 2002). Initial cable and DSL installations also required a visit from a service representative, and there is a general consensus that these costs slowed availability and access did not keep up with consumer demand (Greenstein and Prince, 2007; Faulhaber, 2002).[9] News media reports are indicative that potential subscribers often faced long wait times for installation.[10]

The fact that residential broadband deployment lagged consumer demand provides a potential source of exogenous variation in home Internet adoption. Information on access, however, would be problematic as an instrumental variable because ISPs may have partially responded to consumer demand for home Internet services in determining where to provide access. If trends in latent consumer demand for Internet services are systematically correlated with trends in labor supply, access itself would not satisfy the exclusion restriction.

When installing residential high-speed Internet, existing wiring within a home or building generally does not need to be upgraded for either cable-based or DSL Internet. What needs to be upgraded is the wiring that connects the home or building's existing indoor lines to the ISP.[11] From the ISP's perspective, this made certain types of residences easier and more

---

[9]Some scholars arguer that availability was not driven by consumer demand for home high-speed Internet connections at all. Faulhaber (2002) argues that cable companies upgraded lines under pressure to keep up with satellite TV competition and the phone companies simply followed suit.

[10]See, for example, "Broadband: What Happened?" Businessweek 6/11/01 (Rosenbush et al., 2001)

[11]Both cable-based and DSL broadband Internet service requires the installation of fiber-optic wiring, which provides high-speed Internet service up to a certain point, from which the signal travels over traditional coaxial cable or copper telephone wiring the rest of the way. These fiber-optic lines may reach the ISPs central office, some remote terminal in the neighborhood, the "curb", or the "demarcation point" (see figure 1). The main issue that prevented timely roll-out for the cable companies was capacity. Cable companies had installed some fiber lines in the 1980s to provide digital cable service, but each additional customer on a single fiber line reduces the "downstream" capacity, meaning that multiple simultaneous users reduces speeds and could exhaust the system. Thus, in order to provide reliable, high-speed Internet service cable

profitable for installation than others. In particular, apartment buildings and other multiple family properties, collectively referred to here as "multiple dwelling units" (MDUs), were preferable to single family homes. Figure 2 illustrates the difference between the two types of connections. For an MDU, each length of upgraded wiring that is installed will service multiple customers, allowing for economies of scale and making it easier and more cost effective to provide each potential customer with access. Moreover, since the ISP or MDU owner usually held the property rights to the "home run" wiring within the building, the ISP obtained de facto monopoly rights to service all families after installation.[12] With these differences in mind, I propose that areas with more MDUs should have received Internet access earlier than areas with less MDUs.[13]

Information on local MDU rates was collected from the 2000 Decennial Census, which records population totals in different types of housing units based on the number of units in the structure. A recent Federal Communications Commission (FCC) ruling defines a MDU as "... a multiple dwelling unit building (such as an apartment building, condominium building or cooperative) and any other centrally managed residential real estate development

---

companies needed to add more fiber lines which came closer to residences. For DSL Internet from the phone companies, roll-out was prevented by the need to upgrade the existing telephone wiring, much of which was old and had been split too often to be capable of carrying high-speed two-way traffic. The key insight is that in either case, existing wiring within the home was of sufficient quality to provide individuals with access, while much of the wiring outside the home was not. A more detailed description of high speed Internet deployment and installation can be found in the appendix.

[12]When the MDU owner held the property rights on wiring, the ISP would often offer him a discounted personal connection or incentives to recruit tenants. Before 2007, if the ISP held the rights to the wiring the ISP had a monopoly. In 2007, the FCC issued a ruling aimed at encouraging competition within MDUs by forcing ISPs who owned wiring to share with competing firms. In practice, there is some skepticism about whether this policy has been effective and there is anecdotal evidence that ISPs simply shifted property rights to the MDU owners to maintain a de facto monopoly (F.C.C., 2007).

[13]I am not the first to suggest this type of adoption pattern may exist, as it has been suggested that one reason for South Korea and Hong Kong's relatively high adoption rates is the propensity for the population to live in apartments (Hausman (2002), Stross (2011)). There are also several recent working papers that have proposed identification strategies that exploit alternative supply-side constraints to access. Bhuller et al. (2011) study the impact of the Internet on sex crimes. They use cross-sectional variation in a publicly funded broadband roll-out program in Norway. Falck, Gold, and Heblich (2012) study the impact of the Internet in German elections. They exploit a technological limitation of DSL provision which creates a kink in accessibility at a precise distance from the central office of the telephone company. While this technological feature of DSL provision is also apparent in the U.S., DSL has a considerably lower market share in the U.S. (around 30 percent, as opposed to over 95 percent in Germany). Since this kink is not present in cable-based broadband technology, it would be expected to have little predictive power for overall access rates in the U.S..

(such as a gated community, mobile home park, or garden apartment); provided however, that MDU shall not include time share units, academic campuses and dormitories, military bases, hotels, rooming houses, prisons, jails, halfway houses, hospitals, nursing homes or other assisted living facilities." (47 C.F.R. § 76.2000, 2008). Unfortunately, it is not possible to perfectly map the Census data to this definition, since its not clear from the Census data if a structure like a townhouse or duplex is part of a centrally managed development. Therefore, I looked at several reasonable definitions and chose the one with the most predictive power in the first stage, which was to define an MDU as any unit in a structure with 3 or more units and mobile homes.[14] Results using various alternative definitions are similar and described in the robustness checks. Defining an MDU in this way implies that MDUs constitute about 25 percent of privately occupied residences.

To confirm that places with a higher concentration of MDUs received Internet access earlier than other areas, I examine the relationship between MDU rates and Internet access over time. Data on local high-speed Internet access rates can be obtained from the FCC Form 477 filing data, which has information reported by Internet services providers on zip codes in which they have at least one high-speed Internet customer. I use this information to estimate the unconditional correlation between the share of a state living in an MDU in 2000 and the share of households in a state with high-speed Internet access, separately by year.[15] Figure 4 (a) displays the results, confirming the proposed relationship between the instrument and access rates: a 10 percentage point increase in the share of the state residing in an MDU is correlated with a 3.2 percentage point increase in the state's high-speed Internet access rate in 2000. The magnitude of the correlation declines each year there after to a precisely estimated zero by 2006.

---

[14]Miscellaneous housing units (recreational vehicles, vans, boats, etc) as well as dormitories, jails, prisons, and hotels were excluded from both the numerator and denominator in the construction of this measure.

[15]I aggregate this information to the state-level because that is the geographic unit used in the rest of the empirical analysis. This will be discussed in the following section.

3.3 Empirical Specification

The main empirical approach used in this study is to relate individual home high speed Internet use to labor force supply for married women using linear probability models (LPM) and two stage least squares (2SLS). The main regressor of interest is home high-speed Internet use, which is a combination of an individual-level indicator for whether or not the individual is reported to use the Internet at home and a household level indicator for whether or not the household has a high-speed broadband Internet subscription. I focus on high-speed Internet, versus dial-up, for both conceptual and empirical reasons. First, high-speed Internet is expected to be a more effective replacement for earlier technologies in the production of many of the activities which are expected to affect labor supply decisions. For example, it has been argued that both telework and shopping online were simply not feasible using slower dial-up connections (Hausman et al., 2001; Bittlingmayer and Hazlett, 2002). Second, unlike dial-up Internet, the diffusion of broadband Internet was hampered by supply-side constraints, which is essential for the identification strategy.

The main labor supply outcome variable used in the analyses is an indicator for participation in the labor market. I focus on participation instead of hours in the main analyses because the economic predictions are clearer and interpretation is not encumbered by issues of self-selection into the labor market.[16] However, in the robustness checks, I will additionally estimate the effects on hours, as well as full time status, and various thresholds of hours worked per week. I will also examine employment status in the robustness checks. All labor supply outcomes are asked with regard to labor supply the month of the supplement. In most of the analyses, the sample will be limited to married women aged 18-59 whose husband is present, although single women and men will be investigated in the robustness checks as a comparison.

I relate individual high speed Internet usage to individual labor supply using 2SLS, where

---

[16]While the predicted effect on participation is ambiguous because of the various different ways individuals use the Internet, the predicted effects of Internet usage on hours is further complicated by competing income and substitution effects.

the first stage is a LPM of the impact of the instrument on high speed Internet use:

$$HSI_{ist} = Z_{st}\gamma_1 + X_i\gamma_2 + S_{st}\gamma_3 + \theta_t + \eta_s + \nu_{ist} \qquad (1)$$

HSI_{ist} is a dummy variable for whether or not individual i reports using the Internet in a household with broadband in state s and year t. The instrument, Z_{st} is defined as $Z_{st} = MDU_s * \theta_t$. where MDU_s is the percent of the state's population which resides in a housing unit that is classified as an MDU in 2000. MDU_s is expected to affect home Internet usage via the timing of Internet access, since places with a higher MDU_s received Internet access earlier. Therefore, in the main specification it is interacted with the vector of year fixed effects θ_t to allow the impact to vary separately by year.[17] The main effect of MDU_s only varies at the state level, so it is perfectly correlated with the state fixed effects and cannot be included in the model. Figure 4 (b) displays the results of estimating equation (1), where the x-axis corresponds to year t and the y-axis corresponds to the magnitude of the coefficients γ_1 on each component of the vector $MDU_s * \theta_t$. As expected, there is strong positive relationship between the instrument and Internet usage in the early years of diffusion (relative to 2009), and that relationship declines after 2003.

The second stage equation relates high speed Internet use to labor supply:

$$y_{ist} = \widehat{HSI}_{ist}\beta_1 + X_i\beta_2 + S_{st}\beta_3 + \theta_t + \eta_s + \epsilon_{ist} \qquad (2)$$

where y_{ist} is an indicator for labor force participation for individual i in state s in year t. θ_t are year fixed effects, η_s are state fixed effects and ϵ_{ist} is the error term. State fixed effect η_s and year fixed effects θ_t are included to ensure the estimated coefficient on HSI_{ist} is net of any time-invariant differences across states and national trends in Internet access and participation. Standard errors are adjusted for clustering at the state level.

A vector of individual controls X_i are included to absorb demographic differences in

---

[17] In the robustness checks, I also display the results of interacting MDU_s with a time trend and an indicator for years prior to 2003, both of which produce similar results.

rates of home Internet use and labor supply. The demographic characteristics used include dummy variables for race, age category, education, spouse's education, categories for number and ages of children under 18, metropolitan area status, and central-city status. Education is determined by highest degree of schooling obtained and split into four categories: high school dropouts; high school graduate or GEDs; college dropouts and associates degrees; and Bachelors, masters, professional and Ph.D's. Age and number of children are in categories based on both the number of children (zero, one, two, or three or more) and given the number of children, whether children are under or over age 6 (or both). This flexibly controls for the number of children which need to be looked after, as well as whether any or all children are expected to be in school. Metropolitan area and central-city status are included to control for rural/urban differences in high-speed Internet access and labor supply. Central-city status is included separately from metropolitan area status because suburban and urban residents may have differential rates of participation and access. Spouse's education is included to proxy for non-labor income, as well as spousal Internet take-up rates.

A vector of time-variant state-level controls, S_{st} are included to mitigate concerns that various aspects of the labor and housing market may be correlated with trends in home Internet usage and labor supply. These controls were matched by the individual's state of residence and the year of the survey. Table 2 describes these variables and their sources. They include income per capita, housing prices, population density, unemployment rates, and average wages. Unemployment, income per capita, and average wages control for differences across state and time in the labor market, while housing prices and population density control for differences across state and time in the housing and real estate market that may be correlated with trends in work patterns and home Internet use.

Although businesses adopted the Internet much earlier than households, a potential concern is that Internet use at work could be correlated with local residential Internet access. For example, job creation in "high tech" industries might increase the participation of individuals with Internet skills, who are also likely to have a high demand for home high-speed

Internet access. Thus, I include two measures designed to control for local rates of Internet usage at work: "adoption" and "enhancement", which measure the share of the population in each year employed in industries which use the Internet for each of these purposes. These are constructed from the industry specific measures estimated by Forman, Goldfarb, and Greenstein (2003). Adoption refers to the percent of firms in an industry that use the Internet for any purpose, while enhancement refers to using Internet to enhance business, such as through commercial sales online. These measures are interacted with state-year-industry level employment rates to create a measure of state-year Internet adoption and enhancement rates at work.

The key identifying assumption for interpreting the results of this analysis as causal is that baseline state MDU rates would not have been systematically correlated with subsequent trends in labor supply in the absence of residential broadband Internet diffusion. Certainly, women with preferences for being stay-at-home mothers might choose to live in states with more single family homes. It is therefore imperative that the empirical specification include state fixed effects, so that the estimated relationship between MDU rates, home Internet use, and labor supply will be net of time-invariant differences across states in preferences for housing and work. I also condition on individual-level metropolitan area status and central city status, so that the estimated effect will be net of time-invariant differences in preferences between urban, suburban and rural residents.

Any threat to the identification strategy must come from unobserved variation over time in sorting patterns across states that are related to MDU rates. The vector of time-variant state-level controls are included in the model to capture differential trends in the labor and/or housing market which may be correlated with MDU rates and labor supply. Net of these factors, left-over variation in housing stocks across states is expected to be a function of factors such as historical zoning ordinances, weather, and elevation. The intuition behind the empirical strategy is rooted in how these long-standing differences across locations led to differential *trends* in Internet access.[18]

While there is no direct way to test the exclusion restriction, I can further probe the assumption by conducting a placebo test of the reduced form impact of the instrument on labor force participation *prior* to the availability of high-speed Internet. The intuition behind this exercise is that if a state's MDU rate affects labor supply during a time period in which high-speed Internet was not available, then it must affect labor supply through some other mechanism during that time period. If that were the case, there would be serious doubt that the exclusion restriction would be satisfied during the time period in which high-speed Internet was available. The time period I use for this placebo test is 1990-1997, since the first residential broadband subscriptions became available in 1998 (Faulhaber, 2002). The convenient feature of studying this particular time frame for the placebo test is that both business broadband subscriptions and residential dial-up Internet subscriptions were plentiful, so this analysis should help to shed light on whether or not a violation of the exclusion restriction occurs through one those channels. For example, one could imagine that labor force participation increased in areas with more MDUs because firms in those areas had differential trends in demand for Internet-savvy workers. Since business broadband access and Internet knowledge were already established in this pre-period –but home high-speed Internet was not– this strategy should be able to speak to this type of concern.

Figure 5 (a) displays the results the reduced form analysis graphically for the 1990-1997 period. As a comparison, figure 5 (b) displays the results from the 2000-2009 sample used throughout the paper. The data indicates that for the 1990-1997 period, there is no significant impact of an increase in state MDU rates on participation for any of the years shown (relative to the year 1997) and the point estimates display no clear trend or pattern and remain close to zero. On the other hand, for the sample period used in this study,

---

[18]For example, consider two observably similar cities (similar population, income, average age, and cost of living): Washington, DC and Boston, MA. In Washington, the 1910 building height act does not permit residential buildings above 90 feet (roughly a height so that the capital building can be viewed throughout the city). Because of this law, there are fewer tall buildings in Washington DC. All else equal, this would be predicted to have a relative negative impact on subsequent trends in high-speed Internet diffusion.

coefficients are consistently above zero and statistically different from zero for half of the years shown. Overall, this exercise has uncovered no evidence that state MDU rates have an effect on participation in the time period before high-speed Internet access was available, suggesting that state MDU rates do not affect participation except through their effect on Internet availability.

Since there is little evidence that state MDU rates are correlated with trends in other variables that affect labor supply, the remaining threat to assigning a causal interpretation to the estimated β_1 is the possibility of sorting in response MDU rates due to expectations about future Internet access. To the best of my knowledge, the fact that MDU rates can predict trends in access was (and remains) not well known. I also chose to construct the instrument at the state-level (as opposed to a more disaggregated level like county) because concerns about this type of differential sorting are mitigated by the fact that cross-state migration is relatively low. The potential drawback to employing a measure constructed at a more aggregated level is increased measurement error in the first stage if there is substantial within-state variation in the instrument. This would only be problematic to the extent that it reduces the instrument's predictive power and creates a weak instrument problem. This turns out not to be the case in this data, as first stage diagnostics indicate that the state-level instrument is sufficiently powerful. State is also the most disaggregated geographic unit that is available for all CPS respondents, so an added benefit of constructing the instrument at the state level is the ability to study both urban and rural populations.[19]

---

[19]More disaggregated measures are only available for those living in sufficiently populous cities and counties, thus using city or county as the geographic unit would eliminate individuals living in rural areas from the analysis. In section 4.3 I separately examine urban and rural populations, since individuals in rural areas may stand to benefit more from telework opportunities.

4 Estimation Results

4.1 IV Results

Table 3 displays the results of estimating equations (1) and (2). The first row of table 3 displays the results of a simple linear probability model estimates of equation (2). Column (1) presents the unconditional relationship between Internet usage and participation with no control variables included in the model. This exercise indicates that there is a positive correlation between Internet usage and labor force participation. In column (2) I include state and year fixed effects in the model and the point estimate on Internet usage increases slightly. Columns (3) further includes the full set of demographic controls described table 1, and the estimate diminishes slightly from the one presented in column (2). Finally, column (4) additionally includes the full set of state-level controls described in table 2. This is the most conservative and preferred specification. The estimates indicate that Internet usage leads to a 4.7 percentage point increase in participation. This is close in magnitude to what was found in the previous columns, suggesting trends in Internet usage are not well correlated other individual level or aggregate variables which may affect labor supply.

The results presented thus far do not address the possibility of endogenous selection into Internet usage, so the second row of table 3 estimates the model using the proposed IV strategy. Conceptually, it is not clear ex ante whether the naive LPM estimates will over or understate the causal effect of Internet usage. On the one hand, monthly subscription fees may be cost prohibitive for individuals who do not work, so the LPM estimates might overstate the true impact of Internet use on labor supply. On the other hand, if individuals who work spend less time in the home and place less value on a technology that is only used within the home, or if broadband at work is a substitute for broadband in the home, the LPM estimates might understate the true impact of home Internet use on labor supply.

Column (5) of table 3 estimates the sparse model with only state and year fixed effects. This specification is the equivalent of LPM specification shown in column (2). I do not estimate the IV model using the specification from column (1) because the instrument is an interaction between a time-invariant state-level measure and year fixed effects, so the IV model should not be estimated without the state and year fixed effects. The IV estimate is considerably larger than the LPM estimate, but it is also less precise and the results are not statistically significant at conventional levels. Column (6) additionally includes the demographic characteristics and the IV estimate is only slightly reduced. The fact that the demographic controls do not alter the IV estimate is reassuring since we would not expect the individual level characteristics to be correlated with the instrument unless differential sorting were taking place. Finally, column (7) includes the full set of state controls. Again, the magnitude of the IV estimate falls only slightly. The inclusion of the full set of controls does, however, improve the precision of the IV estimate and it becomes statistically significant at the 10 percent level. In this preferred specification, the first stage F Statistic is above the conventional thresholds for weak identification, indicating the instrument is powerful and relevant.[20] The results displayed in column (7) indicate a sizable 18.6 percentage point increase in the probability of participating in the labor market due to high speed Internet usage. Evaluated at the mean participation rate of 73 percent, this corresponds to a 25 percent increase in participation.

In all of the specifications the instrumental variable estimates are considerably larger than the LPM estimates,. This suggests downward selection bias in the LPM estimate, indicating

---

[20]The F-Statistic employed is the conventional Wald F-Statistic, which is commonly used to to test for weak identification. However, I have employed clustered standard errors and the Wald F-Statistic assumes i.i.d. standard errors. In practice, this means it will tend to over-reject the null of under-identification. Therefore, I have alternatively calculated a "robust" version of the F-Statistic which employs the Kleibergen and Paap (2006) rk statistic, as suggested by Baum, Schaffer, and Stillman (2007). In practice, the two are nearly identical in all specifications and using the Wald F-Statistic does not affect interpretation. Therefore, I will employ the conventional Wald F-Statistic to test for weak identification in the remainder of the paper. The conventional threshold for weak identification has been the rule of thumb of 10, or more appropriately, the Stock-Yogo critical values. Stock and Yogo (2005) provide two methods for evaluating the presence of weak instruments. The first considers the relative bias of IV as compared to OLS, where an instrument is considered weak at x percent if IV has a relative bias of more than x percent. Those critical values are as follows: 5% 16.85 10% 10.27 20% 6.71 30% 5.34. The second considers the Wald test, which rejects too often with weak instruments. An instrument is considered weak at x percent if the Wald Test has a rejection rate of x percent when it should have a rejection rate of 5%. Those critical values for my case are 10% 24.58 15% 13.96 20% 10.26 25% 8.31.

that women who do not work are more likely to take up high speed Internet. However, a key difference between the OLS and IV results is that the IV estimate is a local average treatment effect (LATE), which only applies to marginal Internet adopters – women who are induced into Internet usage by changes in the instrument (Imbens and Angrist, 1994).[21] If there is heterogeneity in treatment effects, so that women who are induced into Internet usage by the instrument are women who can benefit more from its usage, the IV estimate may overstate the overall average causal effect. This selection bias could potentially outweigh any bias in the LPM estimate, in which case case the IV estimate could be farther from the true average causal effect than the LPM estimate. In the next section, I explore this possibility further.

4.2 Heterogeneity and Marginal Treatment Effects

To further explore the IV results, I estimate marginal treatment effects (MTEs) (See, for example, Heckman and Vytlacil, 2001, 2005; Heckman, Urzua, and Vytlacil, 2006). The MTE describes the mean labor market return to Internet usage for individuals who are induced into Internet usage at a particular value of the instrument. Heckman et al. (2006) show that most familiar treatment parameters –including the linear IV LATE and the average treatment effect (ATE)– can be expressed as a weighted averages of MTEs. By estimating the distribution of MTEs, I will be able to see how treatment effects vary across the population and uncover how the IV estimator weights different segments of the population to arrive at the LATE estimate.

To garner some intuition on how the MTEs might be expected to vary as the instrument varies, it is useful to consider the following simple latent index model for Internet take up:

---

[21]In order to interpret the linear IV estimate as LATE the monotonicity assumption must be satisfied. In this case, monotonicity assumes that women who would take up Internet when access rates are low, would also take up when access rates are high. And similarly, those who don't take up Internet when access rates are high also would not do so when they are low. Although untestable, this assumption seems reasonable in this case, since there is evidence that obtaining a subscription in the early years of roll-out was more difficult than it was in later years.

$$HSI* = -B_i + \theta_i$$
$$HSI = 1 \; if \; HSI* > 0$$

Where B_i describes barriers to Internet take-up, such as lack of access or price and θ_i describes an individual's latent level of interest in broadband Internet. A woman uses the Internet when her latent level of interest in the Internet, θ_i is greater than B_i. Some women will have very high $\theta's$ and will almost certainly use broadband Internet. This type of woman would be the first to sign up for installation when wiring reaches her area, or she might even purchase costly satellite or business lined to circumvent a lack of residential access (although in practice, this is extremely rare in the data).[22] Some women will have very low $\theta's$ and will almost never use Internet, whether it is readily available or not. Thus, the marginal adopter of high speed Internet will have a relatively higher average θ_i when B_i is high and a relatively lower average θ_i when B_i is low. Empirically, I will proxy for B_i using the proposed instrument: variation across time and place in access induced by the fraction of the population residing in a MDU multiplied by time.

The estimated MTEs and standard errors are displayed in figure 6 (a), where the MTEs are traced out over the support of the propensity score (the predicted probability of Internet usage conditional on the instrument).[23] Details on how the MTEs were calculated can be found in the appendix. Standard errors are indicated by the dashed lines and were calculated every 5 percentage points using 500 bootstrap replications. Figure 5 indicates that as the propensity score increases, women on the margin of usage display greater labor supply responses to high speed Internet. For the lower half of the distribution of the propensity score, the MTEs are close to zero and even slightly negative, while in the upper half of the distribution the effects are increasingly large and positive. The average MTE for the

---

[22] The CPS asks individuals about their method of access, including dial-up, broadband, and other methods such as business line (T1 line) or satellite. 0.52 percent of Internet users report having T1 or satellite connections between 2000-2007.

[23] The MTEs can only be calculated for values of the propensity score for which there is full support, which in this case ranges from 0.0003 to 0.975.

bottom quartile of the propensity score is -0.125, and the average MTE in the top quartile is almost five times as large at 0.613. This pattern of increasing MTEs is indicative that the labor supply response to high speed Internet increases in barriers to usage, and hence, unobservable interest in Internet services.[24] In other words, women with the greatest latent interest in Internet services also display the greatest labor supply response. This suggests that latent interest may be at least partially determined by private knowledge of expected labor market gains from take-up. Unfortunately, the MTEs are fairly imprecise (especially at the tails) and because of this we can't reject a slope of zero, despite the appearance of substantial heterogeneity.

To further explore the source of the IV estimates, I estimate the weights the linear IV estimator uses to weight the MTEs and produce the linear IV estimate. I estimate the weights directly from the data as described in Heckman et al. (2006) and the appendix to this paper. Figure 6 (b) displays the estimated IV weights and figure 6 (c) displays the population weights as a comparison. The difference between the two distributions indicates that the IV estimator places relatively more weight on individuals with higher values of the propensity score and larger treatment effects. This implies that the IV estimate suffers from positive selection bias: women we expect to be unobservably more interested in Internet services (perhaps because they have higher expected labor market gains) are receiving relatively more weight in the IV estimate.

With the MTEs in hand, it is possible to estimate an average effect of Internet usage on labor supply that does not suffer from the positive selection bias present in the IV estimate. To do so, I simply weight the MTEs by their population weight at each point in the propensity score. This exercise indicates that Internet usage leads to a 6.7 percentage point increase

---

[24]To simplify the analysis, I modify the instrument variables strategy slightly so I have a single instrument $Z_{st} = MDU_s * t$. In practice, this produces almost identical results to the original, more flexible specification with multiple instruments (see section 4.6). Using this specification, the coefficient on Z_{st} in equation (1) is -0.078, because the positive effect of MDU_s declines over time. This means that the x-axis declines in Z_{st}. Figure 4(a) indicates that the instrument has a positive effect on access (although it declines over time), so an increase in Z_{st} corresponds to a decline in B_i. Thus, as $P(Z)$ increases (Z_{st} decreases), and B_i increases.

in the probability of participating in the labor force.[25] Evaluated at the mean rate of participation, this corresponds to a 9.2 percent increase in participation. Because the MTEs are imprecisely estimated, I exercise some caution in interpreting this parameter as a precise estimate of the true causal effect. However, using the MTEs to estimate the linear IV LATE, I estimate an effect of 0.185, which is extremely close the linear IV estimate and provides some assurance that the MTEs can be used to make reliable approximations of other treatment parameters.

4.3 Different Demographic Groups

The evidence presented above suggests that the effects of high speed home Internet usage are heterogeneous and home Internet increases participation for some individuals, while it has little to no effect for others. To get a better grasp of the source of this heterogeneity, I look at which demographic characteristics are associated with large treatment effects. To begin, it is useful to reconsider the conceptual framework outlined in section 2, and consider how the effects might be expected to vary across groups. For example, telework is much more common among more educated individuals: in 2009, 65 percent of teleworkers held a college or postgraduate degree (WorldatWork, 2009). Thus, to the extent that telework opportunities drive part of the estimated net effect one would expect to see a greater labor supply response by individuals with more education. Similarly, if telework reduces some of the costs of paid child care, women with children should be most affected. This might also be expected to vary by age of the child, since working from home is likely to be a more effective replacement for after-school child care than it would be for the care of small children who require more supervision. Telework opportunities may also be more beneficial for individuals who live in

---

[25]This average differs from the conventional ATE parameter. The average calculated here describes the average treatment effect for individuals at the margin of being an Internet user. It is really a local average treatment effect over the support of the propensity score, and to calculate the true ATE parameter would require full support. I could alternatively bound the ATE parameter with the information I have, but I do not carry out that exercise here.

rural areas and face greater distances to travel to work. Lastly, women with children may have greater home production responsibilities than childless women, so time-saving in home production online may be more important for women with children.

To investigate heterogeneity, I begin by performing the linear IV analysis on different sub-samples of married women. Table 4 displays the results of estimating equations (1) and (2) on various sub-samples of married women. Column (1) replicates the overall effect estimated in table 3. Columns (2)-(5) display the results by presence of children. This indicates that the effects of Internet usage on participation are largest for women with children under age 18, for whom there is a statistically significant 29.3 percentage point increase in participation associated with Internet usage. Within this group, the largest effects are found among women with school-aged children, although none of the results separated by age of child are statistically significant and F Statistics are below conventional levels. The effects for women without children are small and insignificant, and F statistics are above conventional thresholds. Columns (6)-(8) estimate the model by level of education, separately for high school dropouts, women with high school or some college, and college educated women. This indicates that the effects increase with education. While the effects are negative (but imprecisely estimated) for high school dropouts, there is a statistically significant 38 percentage point increase in participation for college educated women.[26] Finally, I compare women who live in a metropolitan statistical area (MSA) to women who do not in columns (9) and (10). In this case, there is no evidence of heterogeneity in the magnitudes of the effects, although the effects are only statistically significant for the larger, urban sample. This is consistent with recent empirical evidence that suggests the propensity to telework is unrelated to commute times (Lister and Harnish, 2011).

Overall, the linear IV estimates suggest that the effects on participation are driven by

---

[26]The F statistic is below conventional thresholds for high school drop outs and college educated women. If I alternatively split the sample into two groups: high school or less and some or more college (not shown in the table), the results confirm this pattern of increasing point estimates by level of education and F Statistics are above conventional thresholds. Results for the high school or less group are small and statistically insignificant while the results for the some college or more group are large and statistically significant.

women with children (particularly school-aged) and women with high levels of education. But an important caveat for interpretation of this heterogeneity is these estimates face the same potential selection bias as the overall linear IV estimate: the women (within each group) who are induced into Internet usage by the instrument may benefit more from its usage. It is therefore difficult to interpret whether these effects are representative of differential treatment effects or differential selection into Internet usage.

To separate the potential effects of positive selection from heterogeneity in treatment effects I alternatively examine the average observable characteristics of individuals in different parts of the distribution of the propensity score. This exercise will illuminate which demographic characteristics are correlated with large or small treatment effects. Table 5 displays summary statistics for married women in various parts of the distribution of the propensity score. Column (1) displays the mean of each characteristic for the entire sample of married women. Column (2) displays the mean for the first quartile of the propensity score (where treatment effects are small and slightly negative) and column (5) for the fourth quartile of the propensity score (where treatment effects are large and positive). Columns (3) and (6) display the difference between the mean in the specified portion of the distribution of the propensity score (columns (2) and (5)) and the overall mean (column (1)). Columns (4) and (7) displays these differences as a percent of the overall mean.

This exercise provides a clear picture of heterogeneity across many dimensions. The overwhelming difference is due to education, confirming the linear IV results in table 4. Women in the top quartile of the propensity score (where the average effect of Internet usage on participation is 61 percentage points) are 74 percent more likely to have a college education than the average women. They are also 9.2 percent more likely to have children (and 12.6 percent more likely to have school school-aged children). This is also consistent with the results in table 4. Women in the first quartile of the propensity score (where the average effect of Internet usage on participation is -12.5 percentage points) are 55 percent more likely to be a high school dropout, and 3.3 percent more likely to be childless. Women in the fourth quartile are also slightly more likely to live in a metropolitan area. I also examined additional characteristics including spouse's education, race, and age. There is little difference on age, but significant heterogeneity on spouse's education and race/ethnicity. These are unconditional means, however, and since there is no *a priori* reason to expect these characteristics to be related to the treatment effect, they likely reflect the fact that the aforementioned characteristics are highly correlated with level of education.

4.4 Extensions and Robustness Checks
4.4.1 Hours

Internet usage could affect labor supply on the intensive margin as well as the extensive margin, and the size and even direction of the the effects are not necessarily the same. In the neo-classical labor supply model changes in the wage have an unambiguous prediction for participation decisions, but lead to competing income and substitution effects in the hours decision. Moreover, interpretation of the effects on hours is made more difficult by self-selection into the workforce. If new labor market entrants are more likely to work part time, hours of work for the average participant might decline even if hours for those who were already working prior to high speed Internet increased. While it is fairly standard to use selection correction methods to overcome this problem, employing such methods in an IV strategy is difficult. I therefore choose to simply estimate the effect of Internet usage on hours conditional on working, with the caveat that any observed change in hours could be a compositional effect.

Table 6, panel A displays the results. Column (1) displays the results for hours worked per week, indicating that Internet usage leads to a 8.5 hour increase in hours worked per week, which is statistically significant at the one percent level. Column (2) estimates the effects when the outcome is an indicator for whether or not an individual reports working full time, which is defined as working 35 or more hours per week, which indicates there is about a 20 percentage point increase in the probability of working full time, although this is imprecisely estimated and not statistically different from zero.[27] At the mean, this corresponds to a 26 percent increase, which is similar to the estimated effect on hours. Columns (3) and (4) look at the propensity to work 25 or more hours and 50 or more hours. The coefficient on working 25 or more hours is not statistically different from zero, but is also similar in magnitude to the previous findings. The results in column (5) for working 50 or more hours diverge: they indicate that Internet usage increases the propensity to work 50 or more hours per week by 16.8 percentage points, which is a quite sizable effect since the mean is just 10 percentage points. As in the participation results, caution should be used in interpreting these estimates since they apply only to marginal Internet adopters and may over-select those who can benefit most. Nevertheless, they suggest that Internet usage increases hours and full time work among working individuals, with the strongest effects found on working 50 or more hours per week. This is indicative that new entrants to the workforce are those who work above average hours, and/or previously working individuals increased their hours upon taking up home Internet.

4.4.2 Employment

I additionally estimate the effect of Internet usage on employment to determine whether the estimated effects can be attributed to increases in employment and/or unemployment. If Internet usage facilitates job search, it may induce individuals to transition from non-participation to unemployment. This is a very different story than that of women transitioning from non-work to work. Column (5) displays the results for the outcome employment status. The estimate is very similar in magnitude to the estimated effect on labor force participation, suggesting the effects estimated for labor force participation can be interpreted as women entering the labor market to work. The results using the outcome unemployment

---

[27]This outcome is recorded for some individuals who do not report exact usual hours worked, so the sample size is slightly larger than the hours sample.

(not shown in the table) confirm this result and indicate that Internet usage is associated with small and insignificant increases in unemployment. Thus, I interpret the estimated relationship between Internet usage and labor force participation as a reflection of increased entry into the labor force to work.

4.4.3 Robustness Checks

I implement a number of robustness checks on the specification and data construction. Table 6 panel B tests the sensitivity of the estimates to the construction of the instrument. Column (1) presents the results from interacting MDU rates with a time trend (t) as opposed to year fixed effects. While this specification is less flexible than the main specification, the results are nearly identical to those using year fixed effects (although the estimate is less precise). Column (2) displays the results using a binary instrument based on whether MDU rates are above or below the median (denoted *1[MDU]*) interacted with an indicator for whether the time period is prior to 2003 (denoted *Pre*). Again, the results are similar with this less flexible specification. Columns (3) - (4) of table 6 test the sensitivity of the results to using an alternative definition for an MDU. As described in section 4, it is not possible to perfectly map the FCC's definition of a MDU to what is available in the Census. For the main specification, I chose the one that had the largest first stage F statistic: dwellings with 3 or more units. Alternatively, column (3) defines an MDU as dwellings with 2 or more units in the structure and column (4) defines an MDU as a dwelling with 5 or more units in the structure, both interacted with year fixed effects as in the main specification in equation (2).[28] In each case the results are similar to using the original definition.

Finally, I examine the sensitivity of the results to using a different IV strategy. Stevenson (2009) employs an instrument based on lagged state-level consumer demand for technology in her study of Internet job search. The motivation for this strategy is the observation that

---

[28] Note that Census records population totals by units in structure in categories. These are the two closest categories to the original definition.

state technology take up is highly correlated over time and states that were early adopters of previous technologies tend to be early adopters of new technologies (Skinner and Staiger, 2007). The specific measure she uses is an interaction of take-up of automatic washing machines and telephones in 1960 (both constructed from the 1960 decennial census) with time. *Ex ante*, we would not necessarily expect this strategy to produce the same results as those found using the IV strategy used in this paper. First, since the estimates are LATE, they necessarily depend upon the instrument chosen and results might vary simply because they identify effects for different subsets of the population. Second, if there is some contemporaneous technology diffusing alongside the Internet that affects labor supply, this instrument could potentially capture those effects (this would, however, be a violation of the exclusion restriction). Nevertheless, table 6, column (5) display the results re-estimating the original specification using this alternative instrument. The point estimate is similar and easily within 95 percent confidence intervals of the estimated found using the instrument used throughout this paper.

In panel C, columns (1)-(3) I implement various checks on the sensitivity of the results to the inclusion of several alternate control variables. One potential concern is that the included control variables do not accurately control for the right local labor market conditions. For example, the relevant wage might be the female wage rate (as opposed to the overall wage). On the other hand, if labor force participation rates affect wages in equilibrium, the male wage will be more exogenous to the labor supply supply trends. In addition, the appropriate local labor market might be the MSA as opposed to the state. Recall, I construct the instrument at the state to mitigate concerns about sorting. There is no reason, however, that I cannot construct some of the control variables at a more disaggregated level. Thus, I construct MSA level wages for both males and females from the Current Population Survey and additionally include each in the model. For individuals who do not live in an MSA, I use the rural portion of the state's average wage rates. This is shown in columns (6) and (7) of each panel of table 6. In each case, the results are very similar to the original results.

Another concern is that Internet use is related to technology take-up more generally. This only presents a problem for identification if MDU rates can predict trends in other types of technological diffusion. It may be the case, however, that Internet availability encourages individuals to purchase computers, and computer ownership itself affects labor force participation. Therefore, I re-estimate the model with a control for individual computer usage. Unfortunately, the sample is substantially limited by including this control variable, which is only available in 2000-2003 and is only asked at the household level. Moreover, I do not have an instrument for computer usage, so I am not able to interpret the coefficient on computer usage as causal. Results are displayed in the column (8) of each panel in table 6. Although results are imprecise because the sample is restricted, the point estimate is very similar to the original specification, providing no reason to be concerned about the omission of this control in the main specification.

Finally, I investigate the of impact of high speed Internet on labor supply for single women and men in the columns (9) and (10) of each panel in table 6. Home Internet use should have an impact of individuals who are on the margin of entering the labor market *and* can benefit from working from home, job search, and/or time saving in home production. Since single female and male labor force participation rates historically been relatively inelastic, there is less *a priori* reason to think that home Internet use should impact these group's labor supply. Moreover, many of the potential mechanisms discussed in the conceptual framework are potentially less relevant for these groups. For both men and single women, there is no evidence of a relationship between Internet usage and labor supply.

5 Interpreting the Results: Why Has the Internet Changed Labor Supply?

The analysis presented thus far indicates that, on average, home Internet usage leads to an increase in labor market participation for married women, with substantial heterogeneity in the effects of Internet usage across groups. In this section, I examine the mechanisms that can explain this increase, including telework, job search, home production and leisure. The observed heterogeneity in the effects of Internet usage across demographic groups hints at possible mechanisms. Positive treatment effects of Internet usage are associated with having more education and having children at home (especially school-aged children). As discussed in the previous section, telework opportunities are expected to be particularly important for more educated women and those with children. Time saved in home production is expected to be particularly important for women with children. This provides *prima facie* evidence that telework is likely to be a leading explanation, but home production might also play a role.

In order to investigate which mechanism can best explain the results, I compare group-level Internet usage rates for various activities with group-level labor supply responses to high speed Internet, which are available in the CPS from 2000 to 2003. To do so, I estimate group-level predicted changes in labor force participation when home high-speed Internet use increases from 0 to 1, $\widehat{LFP}_g$, and group-level mean rates of Internet use for each of the various tasks $\frac{1}{N_{sg}} \sum_{sg} HSI(task = t)$, where groups are defined by Census division, education and the presence of children. I construct $\widehat{LFP}_g$ by estimating group specific β_1's according to equation (2), and I construct rates of use for each activity conditional upon Internet usage overall. The goal of this analysis is to inform the extent to which Internet use for each activity contributes to the estimated effect. If there is no correlation between rates of use for a task and the predicted effects, this would suggest Internet use for that purpose is not an important driver of the results. On the other hand, a strong positive correlation suggests

Internet use for that purpose may indeed play a role in explaining the results.

Figure 4 displays the results for work, job search, shopping/paying bills (representing home production) and playing games/fun/recreation (representing leisure).[29] Each activity except "games/fun/recreation" is positively correlated with the predicted effects, which is consistent with Internet use for leisure reducing labor supply while Internet use for telework, job search, and home production increasing labor supply.[30] Overall, Internet use for work appears to be the best explanation for the increase in participation, as it displays the strongest positive correlation between usage and $\widehat{LFP}_g$. The coefficient on the line of best fit is 0.19, and a comparison of individuals across the distribution of $\widehat{LFP}_g$ indicates that those in the top quartile are 53 percent more likely to use Internet for work. Internet use for home production and job search also displays positive correlation with $\widehat{LFP}_g$, although they are less strong. This suggests all three mechanisms can explain the results.

I also conducted various additional supplemental analyses into each mechanism separately which are described in the appendix. I employed data on Internet usage, telework, employment histories and time use to examine the relationship between telework patterns and Internet usage, the effect of Internet job search on durations of transitions from non-participation to participation, and compare the amount of time Internet users and non-users spend in home production tasks. I find that occupation-level average rates of telework and home Internet usage are highly correlated, but Internet usage cannot predict propensities to self-employed or telework full time. This is consistent with home Internet permitting individuals to engage in flexible scheduling arrangements through an employer, which is the type of telework that has grown the most substantially in the past 10-15 years (WorldatWork, 2006,

---

[29]Between 2000 and 2003 the CPS asked respondents about different activities conducted online, although the wording of the questions vary from year to year. Internet use for "work" is defined as use of Internet and email for job related tasks and use of computer to work at home. Internet use for job search was asked consistently over time. To tabulate home production activities, I focused on use of Internet for "shopping/paying bills," which includes use of Internet to shop, pay bills or engage in commercial activities, purchase products and services, and bank online. To tabulate leisure activities I focused on enterainment related activities, including playing games, recreation, enterainment, fun, TV, movies, and radio.

[30]This negative relationship is even more striking when one considers that Internet use for one task is highly predictive of Internet use for other tasks (correlations between tasks range from 0.15-0.3) and is reassuring for the validity of the strategy as a whole.

2009). I also find that Internet job search speeds up transitions from non-participation to participation, and Internet users spend less time in home production tasks than non-users. Overall, the results confirm the correlations found in figure 4: telework, job search and time saved in home production are all plausible mechanisms explaining the results, and the ability to engage in telework appears to be the greatest contributor to the estimated effects.

6 Conclusion

High-speed Internet has changed the way individuals live and work. Using an instrumental variables strategy that exploits supply-side constraints to high-speed Internet access, I find evidence that exogenously determined home high-speed Internet usage leads to increases in labor force participation for married women. The average effects mask substantial heterogeneity in the effects of Internet usage, and larger increases in participation are associated with higher levels of education and the presence of children.

This work speaks to the potential labor market impact of extending high-speed Internet access, and importantly, for whom access is important. More broadly, this paper addresses the labor market effects of the diffusion of a home technology. Unlike technology diffusion in the workplace, which may directly affect productivity, the link between home technologies and labor market outcomes is less clear. Similar to work on the diffusion of time-saving appliances in the twentieth century, I find that female labor supply is sensitive to technological progress in the home sector.

The conflicting demands of work and family force households to make difficult decisions. I find evidence that home Internet can increase labor supply among highly skilled women with families, suggesting home Internet facilitates work-life balance for this group. I also find evidence that telework is a leading explanation for the positive labor supply response to Internet usage. This speaks to broader policy discussions about the potential benefits of telework and flexible scheduling policies. While it is generally accepted that flexibility in the workplace has the potential to benefit employers, employees and the economy as a whole, adoption is still low and there is little empirical evidence on the benefits/costs of these policies.[31] This paper has demonstrated that Internet usage, via take-up of telework opportunities, has allowed a group of highly educated women to join the workforce, suggesting such policies may have the potential to encourage workforce entry by productive individuals.

References

Aguiar, M. and E. Hurst (2007). Measuring trends in leisure: The allocation of time over five decades. *The Quarterly Journal of Economics 122(3)*, 996–1006.

Autor, D. (2001). Wiring the labor market. *Journal of Economic Perspectives 15(1)*, 25–40.

Baker, M. and K. Milligan (2008). How does job protected maternity leave affect mothers' employment and infant health. *Journal of Labor Economics 26(4)*, 655–692.

Baum, C. F., M. E. Schaffer, and S. Stillman (2007). Enhanced routines for instrumental variables/GMM estimation and testing. *Boston College Economics Working Paper 667*.

Becker, G. (1965). A theory of the allocation of time. *Economic Journal 75(299)*, 493–517.

Belkin, L. (2003). The opt-out revolution. *New York Times Magazine October 26*.

Bertrand, M., C. Goldin, and L. F. Katz (2009). Dynamics of the gender gap for young professionals in the corporate and financial sectors. *NBER Working Paper 14681*.

Bertrand, M. and K. Hallock (2001). The gender gap in top corporate jobs. *Industrial and Labor Relations Review 55*, 3–21.

Bhuller, M., T. Havnes, E. Leuven, and M. Mogstad (2011). Broadband internet: An information suprehighway to sex crime? *IZA Discussion Paper Series No. 5675*.

Bittlingmayer, G. and T. W. Hazlett (2002). The financial effects of broadband regulation. In R. H. Crandall and J. H. Alleman (Eds.), *Broadband: Should We Regulate High-Speed Internet Access*, pp. 245–277. AEI-Brookings Joint Center for Regulatory Studies.

Black, D., N. Kolesnikova, and L. J. Taylor (2008). Why do so few women work in New York (and so many in Minneapolis)? *Working Paper*.

Black, D. A., A. M. Haviland, S. G. Sanders, and L. J. Taylor (2008). Gender wage disparities among the highly educated. *Journal of Human Resources 43*, 630–659.

---

[31] See, for example, the report by the Council of Economic Advisers on Work-life Balance, March 2010.

Bloom, N., J. Liang, J. Roberts, and Z. J. Ying (2012). Does working from home work? Evidence from a chinese experiment. *Working Paper*.

Boushey, H. (2005). Are women opting out? Debunking the myth. *CEPR Briefing Paper*.

Brencic, V. (2012). Search online: Evidence from online job boards and resume banks. *Working Paper*.

C.E.A. (2010). Work-life balance and the economics of workplace flexibility. *Council of Economic Advisors Report March 2010*.

Falck, O., R. Gold, and S. Heblich (2012). E-lections: Voting behavior and the internet. *IZA Discussion Paper Series No. 6545*.

Faulhaber, G. R. (2002). Broadband deployment: Is policy in the way? In R. H. Crandall and J. H. Alleman (Eds.), *Broadband: Should We Regulate High-Speed Internet Access*, pp. 223–244. AEI-Brookings Joint Center for Regulatory Studies.

F.C.C. (2007). Exclusive service contracts for provision of video services in multiple dwelling units and other real estate developments, MB Docket No. 07-51, Report and order and further notice of proposed rulemaking, F.C.C. 07-189.

F.C.C. (2008). 47 C.F.R. § 76.2000(b). Exclusive access to multiple dwelling units generally.

F.C.C. (2010). Federal communications commission's broadband internet access page, Accessed february 16 2010.

Forman, C., A. Goldfarb, and S. Greenstein (2003). Digital dispersion: A geographic census of commercial internet use. In S. Craner and Lorrie (Eds.), *Rethinking Rights and Regulations: Institutional Responses to New Communication Technologies*. MIT Press.

Greenstein, S. and J. Prince (2007). The diffusion of the internet and the geography of the digital divide in the united states. In D. Q. Mansell, Robin and R. Silverstone (Eds.), *Oxford Handbook on ICTs*. Oxford University Press.

Greenwood, J., A. Sheshadri, and M. Yorukoglu (2005). Engines of liberation. *Review of Economic Studies 72*, 109–133.

Grubesic, T. H. and A. T. Murray (2002). Constructing the divide: Spatial disparities in broadband access. *Papers in Regional Science 81*, 197–221.

Hausman, J. (2002). Internet-related services: The results of asymmetric regulation. In R. W. Crandall and J. H. Alleman (Eds.), *Broadband*, pp. 129–156. AEI-Brookings Joint Center for Regulatory Studies.

Hausman, J., J. G. Sidak, and H. J. Singer (2001). Residential demand for broadband telecommunications and consumer access to unaffiliated Internet content providers. *Yale Journal on Regulation*.

Heckman, J. J., S. Urzua, and E. Vytlacil (2006). Understanding instrumental variables in models with essential heterogeneity. *The Review of Economics and Statistics 88(3)*, 389–432.

Heckman, J. J. and E. Vytlacil (2001). Local instrumental variables. In C. Hsiao, K. Mormimune, and J. Powell (Eds.), *Nonlinear Statistical Modeling: Proceedings of the Thirteenth Annual Symposium in Economic Theory and Econometrics: Essays in Honor of Takeshi Amemiya*, Cambridge, U.K., pp. 1–46. Cambridge University Press.

Heckman, J. J. and E. Vytlacil (2005). Structural equations, treatment effects, and econometric policy evaluation. *Econmetrica 73(3)*, 669–738.

Herr, J. L. and C. Wolfram (2009). Work environment and 'opt-out' rates at motherhood across high-education career paths. *NBER Working Paper 14717*.

Imbens, G. W. and J. D. Angrist (1994). Identification and estimation of local average treatment effects. *Econometrica 62(2)*, 467–475.

Kleibergen, F. and R. Paap (2006). Generalized reduced rank tests using the singular value decomposition. *Journal of Econometrics 133*, 97–126.

Kroft, F. and D. Pope (2010). Does online search crowd-out traditional search and improve matching efficiency? Evidence from craigslist. *Working Paper*.

Kuhn, P. and H. Mansour (2011). Is internet job search still ineffective? *Working Paper*.

Kuhn, P. and M. Skuterad (2004). Internet job search and unemployment durations. *American Economic Review 94(1)*, 218–232.

Lister, K. and T. Harnish (2011). The state of telework in the u.s.: How individuals business, and government benefit. *Telework Research Network*.

Macunovich, D. J. (2010). Reversals in the patterns of women's labor supply in the united states, 1977-2009. *Monthly Labor Review November*, 16–35.

Rosenbush, S., D. Carney, A. Borrus, T. Lowry, P. Elstrom, C. Haddad, and R. Grover (2001). Broadband: What happened? *Businessweek June 11, 2001*.

Ruhm, C. (2004). How well do parents wtih young children combine work and family life? *NBER Working Paper 10247*.

Sasser, A. (2005). Gender differences in physician pay: Tradeoffs between career and family. *Journal of Human Resources 40*, 477–504.

Skinner, J. and D. Staiger (2007). Technology apoption from hybrid corn to beta blockers. *Hard to Measure Goods: Essays in Honor of Zvi Grilliches*, 545–570.

Smith, A. (2010). Home broadband 2010. *Pew Research Center's Internet and American Life Project*.

Stevenson, B. (2009). The internet and job search. In D. Autor (Ed.), *Labor Market Intermediation*. University of Chicago Press.

Stock, J. H. and M. Yogo (2005). Testing for weak instruments in linear iv regression. In D. W. K. Andrews and J. H. Stock (Eds.), *Identification and Inference for Econometric Models*, pp. 80–108. Cambridge University Press.

Story, L. (2005). Many women at elite colleges set career path to motherhood. *New York Times September 20*.

Stross, R. (2011). Cheap, ultrafast broadband? Hong Kong has it. *The New York Times March 5, 2011*.

Wallis, C. (2004). The case for stayng home. *TIME May 10*, 44.

WorldatWork (2006). WorldatWork 2006 telework trendlines; commissioned from The Dieringer Research Group Inc.

WorldatWork (2009). WorldatWork telework trendlines 2009; Data from The Dieringer Research Group Inc.

Figure 1: Trends in Married Women's Labor Supply 1980-2010

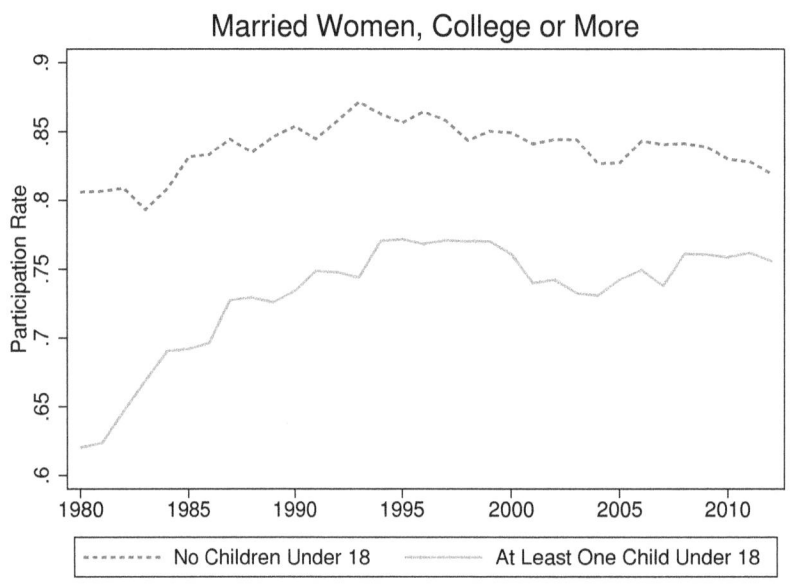

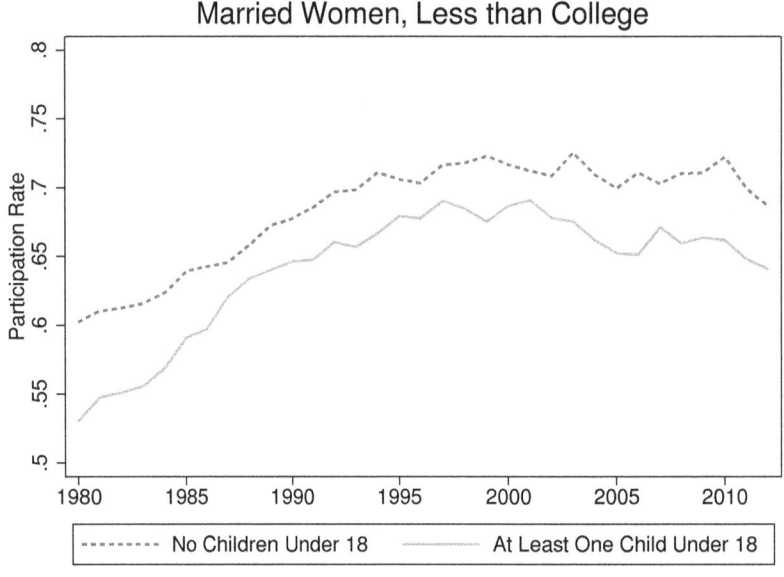

Notes: Displayed are trends in labor force participation rates for married women age 18-59, by level of education and the presence of children, calculated annually from 1980-2010. Source is Annual Social and Economic Supplement (ASEC) of Current Population Survey (CPS). The ASEC supplement weights were used to construct the aggregate counts.

Figure 2: Internet Usage Trends

(a) "Ever Use" the Internet for an Activity

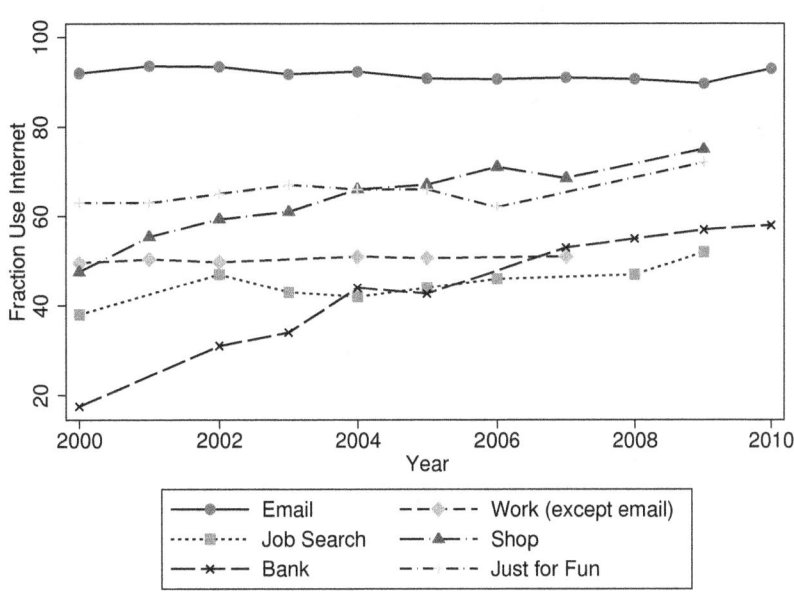

(b) Use the Internet "Yesterday" for an Activity

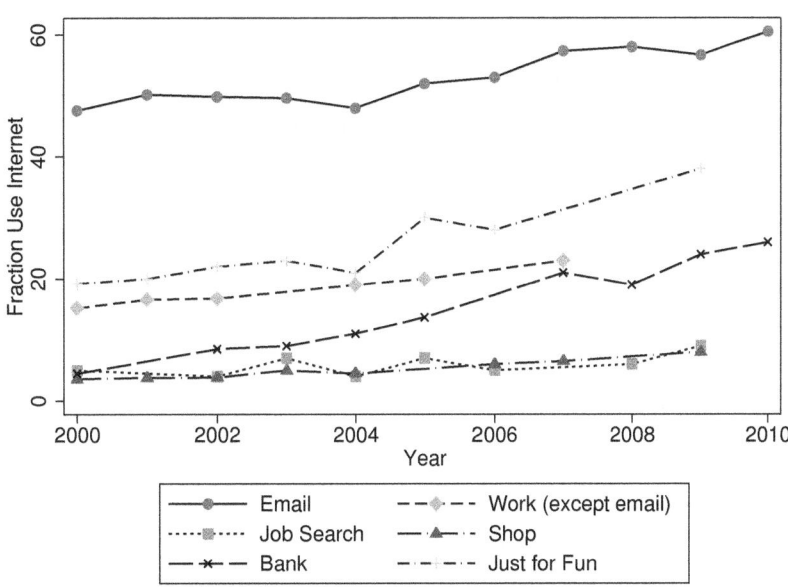

Notes: Displayed are trends in Internet usage for various activities. Data source is PEW Internet and American Life Project "Usage Over Time" trend data (2012).

Figure 3: High-Speed Internet Installation Diagram

(a) Single Family Home

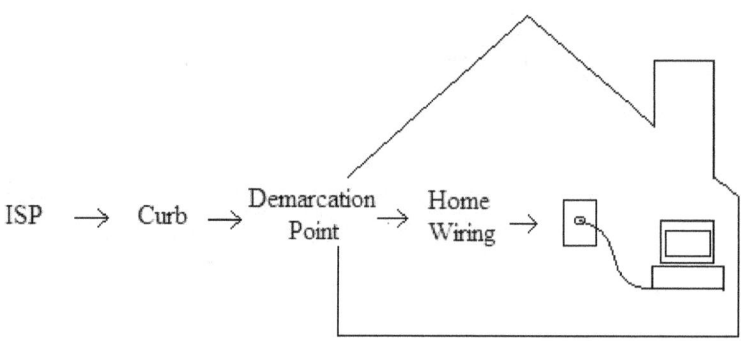

(b) Multiple Dwelling Unit (MDU)

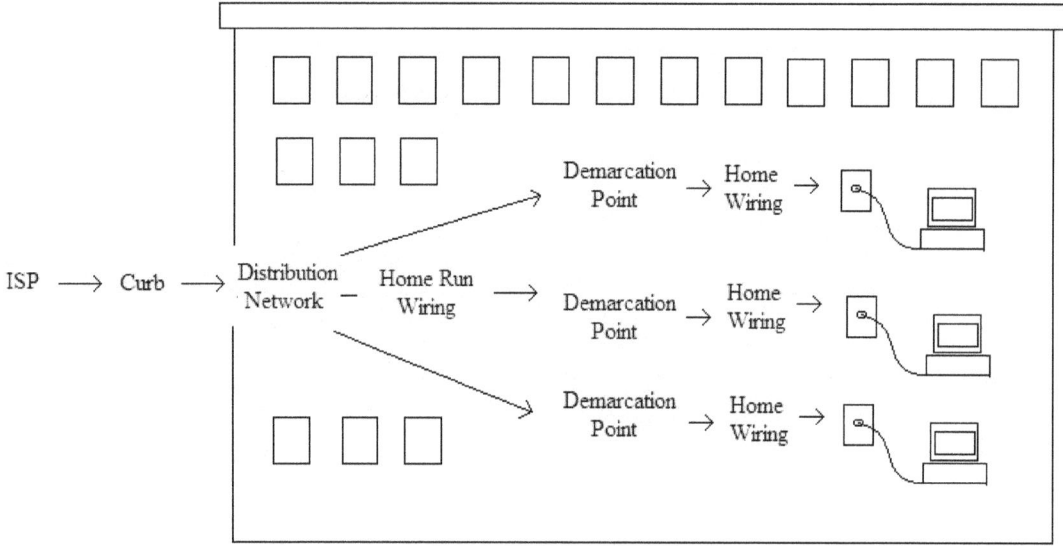

Notes: Author's rendering based on Jackson (2002) and Ames (2006). ISP refers to the high speed Internet service provider.

Figure 4: State MDU Rates and Internet Access and Usage

(a) MDU Rates and Internet Access Rates

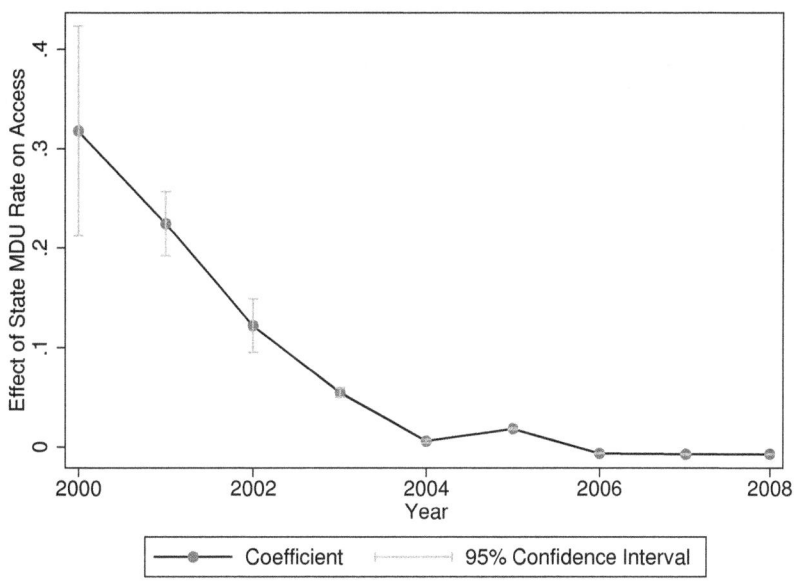

(b) First Stage Coefficients on $MDU_s * \theta_t$

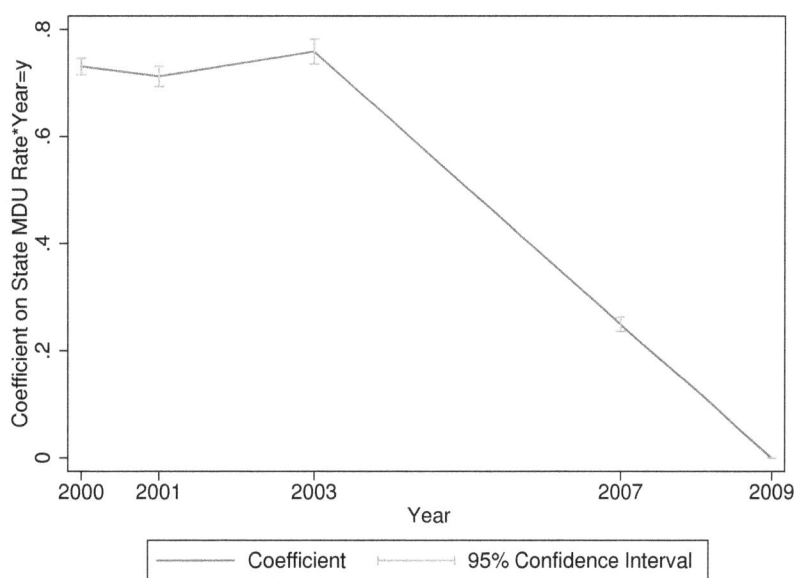

Notes: Panel (a) displays coefficients and 95 percent confidence intervals from a set of unconditional linear regressions relating yearly state-level high-speed Internet access rates to 2000 state MDU rates. Panel (b) displays first stage coefficients and 95 percent confidence intervals on the vector $MDU_s * \theta_t$ for each year t on the x-axis. This was estimated using equation (1), where the outcome is individual high speed Internet usage and coefficients are relative to the base year 2009. Panel (a) includes no control variables, while panel (b) includes state and year fixed effects and the full set of demographic and state-level controls described in the text. Data Sources: (a) FCC form 477 filing data and Census population estimates. (b) CPS Internet supplements and sources described in table 2.

Figure 5: Reduced Form Relationship between MDU Rates and Labor Supply 1990-1997 and 2000-2009

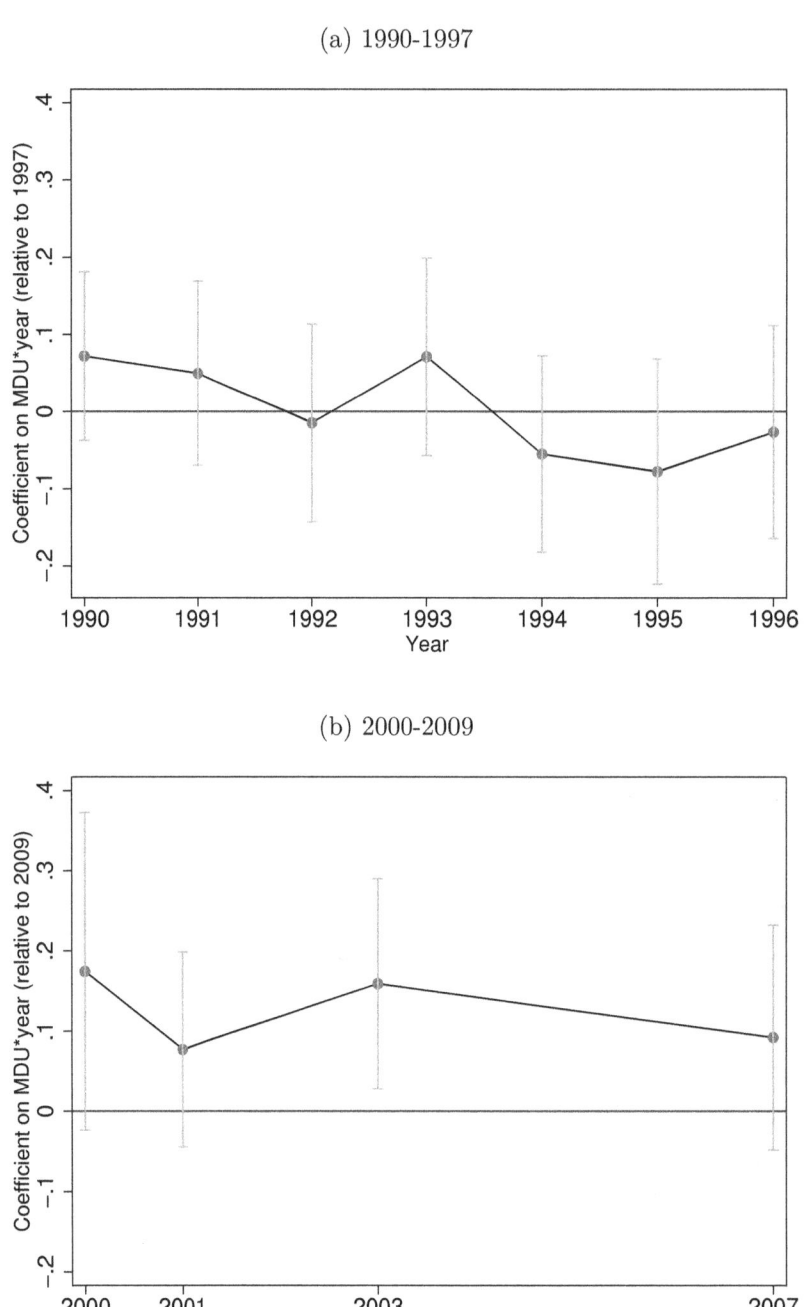

Notes: Displayed are the coefficients and 95 percent confidence intervals on the vector $MDU_s * \theta_t$ from estimation of the reduced form version of equations (1) and (2), which relates the instrument to labor force participation and hours. In panel (a) θ_t=1990-1997 and in panel (b) θ_t=2000, 2001, 2003, 2007 and 2009. Coefficients are relative to the base year of 1997 in panel (a) and 2009 in panel (b). 1990-1997 is the time period prior to the introduction of residential high-speed Internet access and 2000-2009 is the time period used throughout the paper.

Figure 6: Marginal Treatment Effects, IV Weights and Population Weights

(a) MTEs

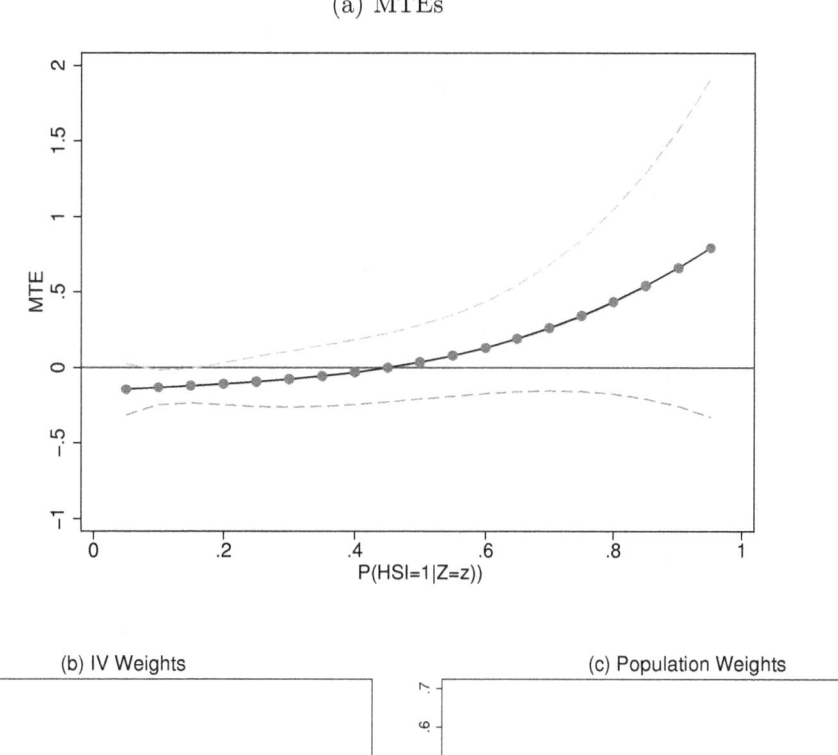

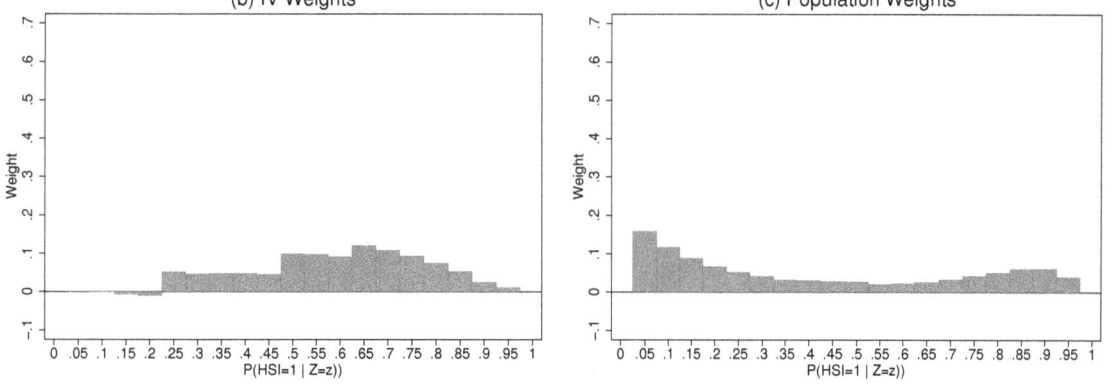

Notes: Panel (a) displays estimated marginal treatment effects (MTEs) of the effect of Internet usage on labor force participation. The solid line represents the MTEs and the dotted lines indicate 95 percent confidence intervals, calculated using a bootstrap with 500 replications at every 5th percentile of the propensity score and clustered at the state level. Panel (b) displays the estimated weights used by the linear IV estimator to weight the MTEs in each part of the propensity score. Panel (c) displays population weights. The weights are calculated in 5 percentage points intervals over the support of the propensity score. Estimation of the MTEs and weights is described in the appendix.

Figure 7: Group Mean Predicted Change in Participation and Rates of Internet Use for Different Tasks

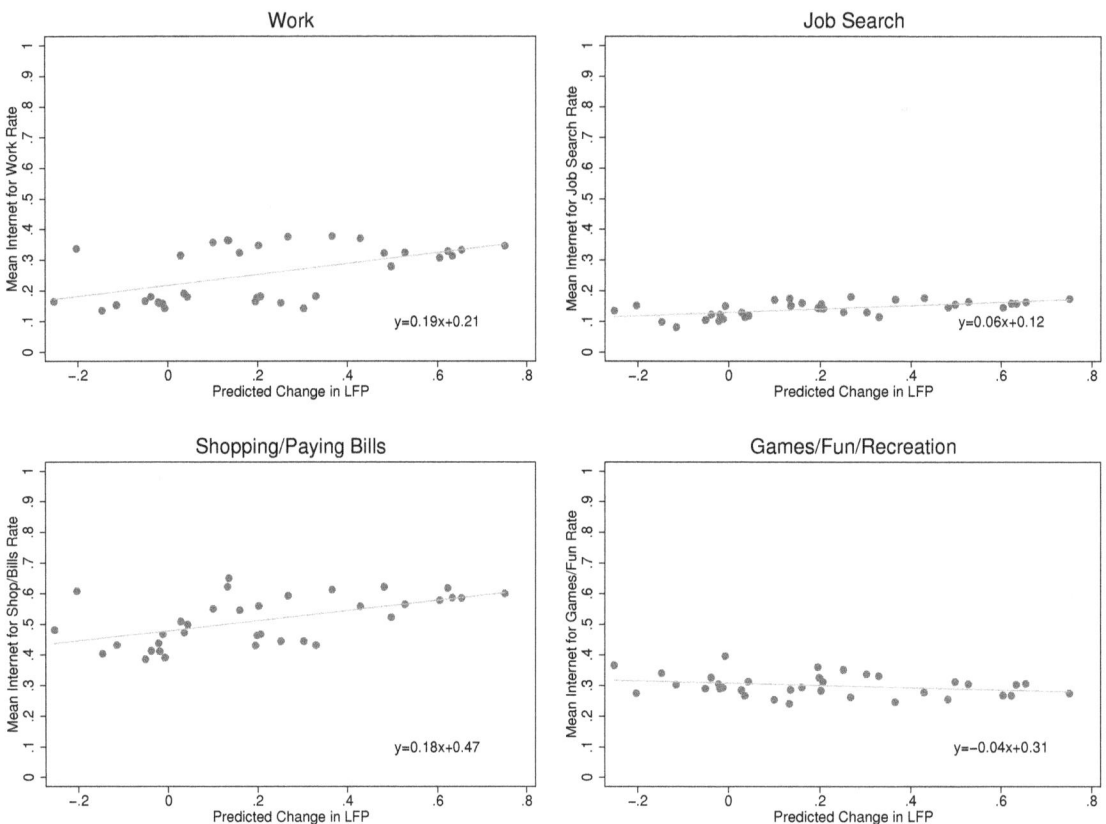

Notes: Plotted is subgroup level mean rates of Internet use for each activity listed and subgroup-level predicted changes in labor force participation when high-speed Internet use increases from 0 to 1 ($\widehat{LFP}$), based on estimating equations (1) and (2) for each subgroup, where subgroups are defined by education, the presence of children and Census divisions.

Table 1: Summary Statistics on Married Women 2000-2009

Variable	Mean	Std. Deviation
High Speed Internet (HSI) User	0.356	0.479
.......in 2000	0.054	0.225
.......in 2001	0.112	0.315
.......in 2003	0.250	0.432
.......in 2007	0.662	0.473
.......in 2009	0.786	0.409
Labor Force Participation	0.731	0.444
Less than High School	0.087	0.282
High School	0.303	0.460
Some College	0.293	0.455
College	0.317	0.465
Spouse-Less than High School	0.103	0.304
Spouse-High School	0.302	0.459
Spouse-Some College	0.265	0.442
Spouse-College	0.330	0.470
Lives in MSA	0.709	0.454
Lives in Central City	0.187	0.390
No Children Under 18	0.454	0.498
One Child Under 18	0.210	0.407
Two Children Under 18	0.218	0.413
3 or More Children Under 18	0.118	0.323
Any Children Under Age 6	0.242	0.428
White (NH)	0.766	0.424
Black (NH)	0.062	0.241
Hispanic	0.106	0.308
Other	0.066	0.249
Age	41.79	10.04

Notes: Displayed are means and standard deviations of the individual level dependent and independent variables from the 2000-2009 Current Population Survey supplements. The sample is limited to married women age 18-59. Full time status and hours worked are conditional upon participation in the labor market. The number of observations is 107,976.

Table 2: Summary of State-Level Variables 2000-2009

	Mean	Description	Source
Income PC	$38,951 ($5,701)	Income per capita	Bureau of Economic Analysis (BEA)
Avg Wage	$43,866 ($7,161)	Average annual wage income per job	Bureau of Economic Analysis (BEA)
Pop Density	135.1 (378.79)	Population density	Census Land Area and Population Estimates
HPI	350.03 (110.57)	Housing price index	Federal Housing Finance Agency (FHFA)
Unemp Rate	5.48 (2.06)	Unemployment rate	Bureau of Labor Statistics (BLS)
Adopt	0.904 (0.066)	Fraction of population working in firm which adopts Internet	Forman et al (2005) and BEA
Enhance	0.129 (0.004)	Fraction of population working in firm which uses internet to enhance business	Forman et al. (2005) and BEA
MDU	0.235 (0.059)	Percent population in multiple dwelling unit	2000 Census

Notes: Displayed are state-level control variables. Income per capita, average wage, and the house price index (HPI) are in 2009 dollars, inflated by CPI-U. Standard deviations displayed in parentheses.

Table 3: Internet Usage and Married Women's Labor Supply

	(1) LPM	(2) LPM	(3) LPM	(4) LPM
HSI Use	0.0670***	0.0903***	0.0471***	0.0471***
	(0.00571)	(0.00824)	(0.00481)	(0.00480)
State and Year FEs	No	Yes	Yes	Yes
Demographic Controls	No	No	Yes	Yes
State-Year Controls	No	No	No	Yes
Observations	107976	107976	107976	107976

	(5) IV	(6) IV	(7) IV
HSI Use	0.215	0.204	0.186*
	(0.145)	(0.144)	(0.0964)
State and Year FEs	Yes	Yes	Yes
Demographic Controls	No	Yes	Yes
State-Year Controls	No	No	Yes
First Stage F Statistic	10.22	12.42	22.64
Observations	107976	107976	107976

Notes: Demographic variables include fixed effects for age category, race, number and ages of children, living in an MSA, and living in a central city. State-level variables include average wages, income per capita, unemployment rates, housing prices, population density, percent of state employees' industry internet adoption and enhancement and are matched at the state-year level. The instrument is percent of state living in a multiple dwelling unit (MDU), interacted with the year fixed effects and is matched at the state-level. Standards errors adjusted for clustering at the state level are in parentheses. * $p < .1$, ** $p < .05$, *** $p < .01$.

Table 4: Instrumental Variable Estimates of Impact of Internet Usage on Labor Force Participation, by Demographic Group

	(1) All	(2) No Children	(3) Child <18	(4) Child <6	(5) Child 6-18
HSI Use	0.186*	0.0276	0.293**	0.176	0.302
	(0.0964)	(0.0979)	(0.145)	(0.129)	(0.236)
Mean Dep. Var.	0.73	0.76	0.71	0.63	0.78
F Statistic	22.64	20.93	16.22	12.18	9.89
N	107976	48745	59231	26128	33103
	(6) Less than HS	(7) High School	(8) College	(9) Not in MSA	(10) In MSA
HSI Use	-0.136	0.229	0.380*	0.176	0.176*
	(0.428)	(0.170)	(0.223)	(0.204)	(0.0913)
Mean Dep. Var.	0.50	0.73	0.79	0.76	0.72
F Statistic	1.93	20.81	6.82	2.13	15.31
N	8999	64210	34767	31293	76683

Notes: Demographic variables include fixed effects for age category, race, number and ages of children, living in an MSA, and living in a central city. State-level variables include average wages, income per capita, unemployment rates, housing prices, population density, percent of state employees' industry internet adoption and enhancement and are matched at the state-year level. The instrument is percent of state living in a multiple dwelling unit (MDU), interacted with the year fixed effects and is matched at the state-level. Standards errors adjusted for clustering at the state level are in parentheses. * $p < .1$, ** $p < .05$, *** $p < .01$

Table 5: Demographic Characteristics of Married Women by Quartile of the Propensity Score

	All	First Quartile			Fourth Quartile		
	(1)	(2)	(3) =(2)-(1)	(4) =(2)-(1)/(1)	(5)	(6) =(5)-(1)	(7) =(5)-(1)/(1)
	Mean	Mean	Difference	% Change	Mean	Difference	% Change
No Children	0.451	0.466	0.015	3.3	0.401	-0.051	-11.2
Children	0.549	0.534	-0.015	-2.7	0.599	0.051	9.2
Children Under 6	0.242	0.242	0.000	0.2+	0.254	0.012	4.9
All Children 6-18	0.307	0.292	-0.015	-5.0	0.346	0.039	12.6
Less than HS	0.082	0.127	0.045	54.9	0.000	-0.082	-99.7
High School	0.596	0.659	0.064	10.7	0.440	-0.155	-26.1
College	0.322	0.214	-0.109	-33.7	0.559	0.237	73.5
Lives in MSA	0.711	0.669	-0.041	-5.8	0.798	0.087	12.3
Spouse-Less than HS	0.099	0.148	0.049	49.2	0.004	-0.095	-95.5
Spouse-High School	0.566	0.617	0.051	9.1	0.440	-0.126	-22.2
Spouse-College	0.334	0.234	-0.100	-30.0	0.555	0.221	66.0
White (NH)	0.776	0.744	-0.031	-4.0	0.859	0.084	10.8
Black (NH)	0.058	0.068	0.010	17.4	0.032	-0.026	-45.0
Hispanic	0.101	0.129	0.028	27.9	0.027	-0.074	-72.8
Age	41.894	41.660	-0.234	-0.6	41.782	-0.112	-0.3+

Notes: Displayed is the mean of an indicator for each demographic characteristic for the specified portion of the distribution of $P(HSI=1|Z=z)$. The exception is age, which is displayed as the mean age in specified portion of the distribution. Means in columns (2) and (5) are significantly different from the mean in (1) at the one percent level except where noted with a +.

Table 6: Extensions and Model Specification Checks

Panel A: Alternative Dependent Variables

	(1) Hours Per Week	(2) Full Time	(3) Hours>25	(4) Hours>50	(5) Employed
HSI Use	8.513***	0.198	0.185	0.168**	0.175*
	(3.242)	(0.132)	(0.116)	(0.0853)	(0.0951)
Mean Dep. Var	37.51	0.54	0.61	0.07	0.70
F Statistic	15.24	19.35	15.24	15.24	22.92
N	70018	76066	70018	70018	107976

Panel B: Alternative Instruments

	(1) Z=MDU*t	(2) Z=1[MDU]*Pre	(3) MDU=2+ Units	(4) MDU=5+ Units	(5) Z=1960 Appliances
HSI Use	0.184	0.240*	0.194**	0.222*	0.130*
	(0.117)	(0.136)	(0.0988)	(0.114)	(0.0739)
F Statistic	54.45	13.54	8.28	19.88	11.00
N	107976	107976	107976	107976	107976

Panel B: Alternative Controls, Different Groups

	(1) MSA Female Wages	(2) MSA Male Wages	(3) Computer Usage	(4) Single Women	(5) Men
HSI Use	0.181**	0.191**	0.158	-0.256	-0.0438
	(0.0762)	(0.0786)	(0.389)	(0.173)	(0.0927)
F Statistic	11.95	12.67	1.37	2.60	8.57
N	76683	76683	68273	79679	178579

Notes: Demographic variables include fixed effects for age category, race, number and ages of children, living in an MSA, and living in a central city. State-level variables include average wages, income per capita, unemployment rates, housing prices, population density, percent of state employees' industry internet adoption and enhancement and are matched at the state-year level. Except where noted othewise, the instrument is percent of state living in a multiple dwelling unit (MDU), interacted with the year fixed effects and is matched at the state-level. Standards errors adjusted for clustering at the state level are in parentheses. * $p<.1$, ** $p<.05$, *** $p<.01$

Appendix

Appendix A: High Speed Internet Deployment

In this section I briefly review broadband network architecture, the history of high speed Internet deployment and how it relates to my empirical strategy. For a more detailed description of broadband technology deployment see, for example, Jackson (2002). There are two fundamental ways that high speed Internet service reaches the customer: cable-based services and DSL services over telephone lines. For both of these services, fiber-optic lines provide high speed Internet service up to a certain point and traditional coaxial cable or copper telephone lines carry service the rest of the way. These fiber-optic lines may reach the ISPs central office, some remote terminal in the neighborhood, the curb, or reach all the way to the home. Connections are often labeled according to this fiber end-point as "fiber to the ... (curb/home/etc.)" (Jackson, 2001). Once the line reaches the residence, wiring inside the home is the property of the home owner (Ames, 2006). The coaxial cable/telephone lines inside the home do not need to be upgraded to receive broadband (they can be upgraded, but in the time period studied this was very uncommon).

Cable companies began developing networks which expanded fiber to neighborhoods (and coaxial cable wiring the rest of the way) beginning in the 1980s. These networks were used to provide digital cable television. This existing system was theoretically capable of simultaneously providing both digital cable and high speed Internet, but each additional customer on a single fiber line reduces the "downstream" capacity, so that if many individuals use Internet/cable at the same time capacity would be exhausted. The networks that were put in place in the 1980s had sufficient capacity to provide most customers with digital cable, but the spread of broadband was not anticipated and the networks were not of sufficient scope to provide both digital cable and high speed Internet during peak hours. Thus, to expand service cable companies needed to extend fiber lines closer to homes. For DSL, providers were able to take advantage of existing capacity in copper telephone wires that were not used for voice services. However, this was limited by distance of the wire and wire quality.

In practice, many providers had to upgrade their local systems to provide consumers with DSL access (Jackson, 2002).

These limitations meant that both cable and DSL companies had to make significant infrastructure investments to keep up with the rapid growth in demand for high speed Internet services. The cable companies had to invest in bringing fiber lines closer to the home and the the phone companies had to deal with wire quality issues. Both had to send service representatives to the home for the first installation, and there were reports of fairly significant wait lists for these visits (Faulhaber, 2002). All of this meant that supply lagged demand, particularly in the early years of roll-out.

Simple intuition indicates that Internet service providers would have had an incentive to choose which markets to enter carefully in order to reach as many potential consumers as possible as quickly as possible. There is evidence that this type of cherry picking did in fact occur, and in the early years of diffusion Internet service was offered to areas with high predicted rates of take up (e.g., high income areas). This source of variation in timing, however, is likely to be correlated with labor market outcomes and would therefore prove unsuitable for an instrumental variables strategy. My strategy will instead focus on the *costs* of providing service to local markets. Recall that both cable and DSL service required investment in upgrading/extending wiring closer to the dwelling. From there, the dwelling owner was responsible for wiring inside the home. In most cases this would not need to upgraded since most homes had cable and phone wiring by the 2000s. Note that this was the case for both a single family home and a multiple dwelling unit (such as an apartment building), since the building owner would have owned the wiring that distributes Internet to each unit within the building. This means that from the ISPs perspective, providing service to a multiple family dwelling with multiple potential customers was quicker and more cost effective than providing service to single family homes with just one potential customer. Thus, all else equal, the ISP would have been able to more quickly and cost effectively provide access in markets with relatively more multiple family dwellings. This is the source of exogenous variation I use to isolate the causal effect of Internet on labor supply.

Appendix B: Marginal Treatment Effect (MTE) Estimation

This section reviews how the marginal treatment effects were estimated, which closely follows the web appendix to Heckman et al. (2006).[1]

The basic framework employed in this paper for estimation of the effect of Internet usage on labor supply can be described as follows: $Y = \alpha + HSI\beta + X\delta + \epsilon$, where X are the observable characteristics of individuals and ϵ are unobservable characteristics. Re-writing this equation in terms of potential outcomes implies the following: $Y_1 = \alpha_1 + \beta + X\delta_1 + \epsilon_1$ and $Y_0 = \alpha_0 + X\delta_0 + \epsilon_0$. Let $HSI = \gamma Z + \nu$ describe the first stage relationship, where Z are the observable characteristics of individuals (including the observables X and the instrument J) and ν are the unobservable characteristics. Then the propensity score is $P(HSI = 1|Z = z) = P(z)$ and the treatment effect of Internet usage can then be expressed as follows:

$$E(Y|X = x, P(z) = p) = \alpha_0 + (\alpha_1 - \beta - \alpha_0)p + x\delta_0 + ((\delta_1 - \delta_0)x)p + K(p)$$

$$K(p) = \beta p + E(\epsilon_0|P(z) = p) + E(\epsilon_1 - \epsilon_0|HSI = 1, P(z) = p)p$$

The MTE is the derivative of $E(Y|X = x, P(z) = p)$ with respect to p, so we can express the MTE as:

$$\frac{\partial E(Y|X = x, P(z) = p)}{\partial p} = (\alpha_1 - \beta - \alpha_0) + (\delta_1 - \delta_0)x + \frac{\partial K(p)}{\partial p}$$

In what follows, I describe how I estimate this parameter.

---

[1] The appendix can be found at http://jenni.uchicago.edu/underiv/documentation_2006_03_20.pdf. Accessed August 2013.

First, I estimate the propensity score by estimating equation (1) using a probit model. For each individual in the sample, the propensity score is the predicted probability of treatment. I use probit so that predicted probabilities are ensured to lie in the [0,1] interval. To simplify the analysis, I modify the instrument variables strategy slightly so I have a single instrument $Z_{st} = MDU_s * t$. Although this specification is less flexible, in practice it produces almost identical results to the original specification (see section 4.6). Support for the propensity score is obtained for values of *P(z)* for which there are positive frequencies in both the treated (*HSI=1*) and untreated (*HSI=0*) sub-samples. In practice the MTE can only be estimated for values of *P(z)* for which there is full support, so I must trim the sample accordingly to estimate the MTEs. Appendix figure 1 displays the distribution of P(z) for the treated and untreated sub-samples and indicates there is full support for the propensity score from *P(z)*=0.0003 to *P(z)*=0.975. It may initially seem surprising that support is found for almost the full unit interval, however, it should be noted that this is *not* the support of P(z) conditional on *X*, and part of the reason there is almost full support is variation in *X* across individuals. If I assume seperability and independence between X and the unobservables in the model, investigating the unconditional support of *P(z)* is sufficient.[2]

To estimate the MTEs I need to estimate each component of the expression above. Except for *K(p)*, these can estimated using a simple linear regression. To estimate *K(p)* there are several possibilities, including parametric and semi-parametric techniques, each of which are outlined in detail in the web appendix to Heckman et al. (2006). I chose to approximate *K(p)* using a fourth degree polynomial in *p*. More precisely, I estimate $y_{ist} = \alpha_0 + X_{ist}\delta_0 + X_{ist}P(z)(\delta_1 - \delta_0) + \sum_{i=1}^{4} \theta_i P(z)^i$ (note that θ_1 now includes $(\alpha_1 - \beta - \alpha_0)$). Then, the MTE is estimated at various values of *p* by plugging the estimated coefficients into the following expression: $\widehat{MTE}(p) = \widehat{\theta_1} + \overline{X}(\widehat{\delta_1 - \delta_0}) + \sum_{i=2}^{4} i\hat{\theta}_i p^i$. To estimate the population weighted average MTE, I calculate this MTE for each individual in the sample based on their value of *p* and estimate a simple arithmetic mean. Note that this average

---

[2]A potential concern would be that all variation in *P(Z)* is driven by *X* and not the instrument, but that is not the case. There is considerable variation in the instrument across the distribution of P(Z).

is calculated conditional on an individual's p being in the support of the propensity score, so it is not the same as the familiar treatment parameter the "average treatment effect" (ATE). That parameter could be bounded with the information available here, but I do not undertake that exercise since I am so close to having full support.

After I've calculated the MTEs, I calculate the weights used by the linear IV estimator. The formulas for the weights, their derivation and their estimation are described in detail in Heckman et al. (2006). The authors show that the IV weight at each p can be expressed as follows:

$$w_{iv}(x,p) = \frac{E(J|P(Z) > p, X = x) - E(J|X = x))Pr(P(Z) > p|X = x)}{Cov(Z, HSI|X = x)}$$

where J is the scalar instrument. Note that I estimate the weights in five percentage point intervals over the support of the propensity score, and I evaluate the weights at the means of the covariates $\bar{X}$. To estimate the weights I begin by approximating $\hat{E}(J|X = x)$ by regressing $J = \gamma X$, and then calculating $\hat{E}[J|X = x] = \hat{\gamma}\bar{X}$. Next, for each value of p, I approximate $E(J|P(Z) > p, X = x)$ by re-estimating $J = \gamma X$ for each sub-sample where $P(z) > p$. Using those values, I estimate $\hat{E}[J|X = x, P(z) > p] = \hat{\gamma}\bar{X}$. Next, I estimate $\widehat{Pr}(P(z) > p|X = x)$ by estimating a linear probability model of $1[P(z) > p|X = x] = \delta X$ and calculating the predicted probability $\widehat{Pr}(P(z) > p|X = x) = \widehat{\delta X}$. I repeat these exercises at every fifth percentage point p in the distribution of $P(z)$ over which I have full support. Then, using the fact that the weights must sum to one, I can back out the denominator $Cov(Z, HSI|X = x)$ and estimate the weight at each value of p. To estimate the IV LATE, I multiply the weights by the MTE at each value of p and sum. Note that this LATE and average MTE are approximations at the mean of the other covariates. In order to recover the exact treatment parameters I would need to integrate out the X's, which is an exercise I do not undertake here.

Appendix C Mechanisms

This section reviews the additionally analyses that I undertook to investigate each potential mechanism via which high speed Internet usage affects labor supply, including telework, job search, home production and leisure.

C.1 Telework

To estimate the effect of Internet usage on telework and its relationship to the labor supply results I begin by investigating summary data on work schedules. This information can be found in the CPS Work Schedule Supplements from 2001 and 2004 and summary statistics for these data are displayed in appendix table 1. Overall, about 24 percent of married women report working at least some hours in the home. Women have a slightly higher propensity to work from home than men, and they work slightly more days/hours in the home when they do so. The average woman who works from home does so approximately 3.5 days per week, 1.2 of which are spent working from home exclusively (i.e., not going into an office at all). Across groups, college educated women are much more likely to work from home than less educated women, although they do so less intensively. This appears to a product of the type of occupations each type of woman tends to hold. Column (6) indicates that women with children are more likely than any other group to report working from home to "coordinate schedules with family or personal needs." This is direct evidence that working from home is a tool women use to balance the demands of work and family.

Use of the Internet for telework increased substantially between 2000 and 2009.[3] Ideally, to identify the effects of telework, I would directly examine the propensity to work at home and use the Internet. Unfortunately, the CPS Work Schedule data does not ask respondents about their own Internet usage so I cannot make this link using these data alone. As an alternative, I look across occupations in CPS Internet data and the CPS Work Schedule

---

[3]WorldAtWork, an organization that collects detailed data on telework behavior, finds that between 2002 and 2008, telework increased 63 percent (2006; 2009).

data to examine whether or not Internet users tend to have occupations where it is likely the individual can telework. Appendix figure 2 displays the correlation between occupation-specific work at home rates and occupation-specific Internet usage rates and indicates there is a strong, positive relationship.[4] Occupations in the top quartile of the distribution of mean Internet usage rates have work at home rates that are five times higher than those in the bottom quartile. A closer examination indicates that the top occupations in terms of work at home and Internet usage are computer scientists, lawyers and post-secondary teachers.

Next, I look at rates of self-employment and full-time telework with the goal of determining if this change represents a shift to full-time, self employed telework or employer-provided flexible scheduling policies. Self-employment can be found in the CPS data and full-time work at home can be found in the American Communities Survey (ACS) which directly identifies exclusive telework in "means of transportation to work", in which respondents may report "worked at home" as their means of transportation. To look at self-employment, I employ the instrumental variables strategy used throughout the paper. For the full-time telework data, I employ a two sample instrumental variables strategy (Angrist and Krueger, 1992). I use the CPS survey data to estimate the first stage relationship for home Internet use and apply those parameter estimates to the ACS to estimate $\widehat{HSI}$ and the second stage relationship between home high-speed Internet use and full time telework. The results of these exercises (not shown here) indicate that home Internet use has not been associated with an increase in the propensity to be self-employed or work at home exclusively. In fact, home Internet use is associated with a decline in both, with a magnitude of 5.3 and 2.5 percentage points, respectively, although neither are statistically significant at conventional levels.[5] These results are consistent with the CPS work at home data presented earlier,

---

[4]The CPS work schedule data is available in 2001 and 2004, while the CPS Internet data is available is 2000, 2001, 2003, 2007 and 2009. I construct averages using all available data for each occupation. Since occupation classifications changed dramatically between the 2000/2001 supplements and 2003-2009 supplements, I use the BLS CPS extracts to harmonize occupations over time http://www.nber.org/data/cps_extract.html.

[5]The coefficient on HSI use for self-employment is -0.0525 with a standard error of 0.0432. For full-time telework, the coefficient on HSI use is -0.0252 with a standard error of 0.0179. The standard error for the full-time telework specification was calculated using 500 bootstrap replications.

which indicated that most individual who work at home only do so 1.2 days exclusively. The results are also consistent with patterns in telework over the period studied: between 2006 and 2008 full-time telework rates fell and self-employed telework rates remained flat, while employer-provided "occasional" telework (at least one day per month) increased 123 percent (WorldatWork, 2006, 2009). This suggests that the mechanism via which home Internet has operated to increase labor supply is the ability to engage in flexible scheduling through an employer who permits occasional telework, as opposed to increases in self-employment or transitions to exclusive work at home status.

C.2 Job Search

There is also evidence that the estimated effects can be explained by job search. While there is a growing empirical literature on role of Internet search in affecting unemployment durations, to the best of my knowledge, there is no evidence on the role of search in affecting participation decisions.[6] To estimate the role of search in this outcome, I exploit the longitudinal nature of the CPS sampling frame to look at the post-survey labor market outcomes of respondents who were asked whether or not they used Internet for job search in the initial survey. I construct employment histories for the sample of married women who use Internet at home and do not participate in the labor force and compare the transition from non-participation to participation for home Internet users who use Internet for search to Internet users who do not use Internet for search.[7]

I begin by estimating a linear probability model for the propensity for an individual to be a labor force participant one year after the initial survey. Since the sample is limited to individuals with Internet at home, I do not need to be concerned about the endogeneity of Internet take-up to work patterns and I do not use the instrumental variables strategy

---

[6]For example, Kuhn and Skuterad (2004) find that Internet search increases unemployment durations, while Stevenson (2009) and Kuhn and Mansour (2011) find opposite results.

[7]This includes the CPS supplements from 1998, 2000, 2001, and 2003. I no longer focus on only high-speed Internet, so I am able to use the 1998 supplement which does not separately identify high-speed and dial up users, but does record activities conducted online.

used earlier. However, I do need to be concerned about take-up of job search practices in general, so I include as a control variable an indicator for whether or not the individual was "doing something to look for work in the past 4 weeks." I also include controls for the individuals age, race, ethnicity, age category, presence of children, year of the survey and state of residence. However, there is still a possibility that Internet take-up for job search is endogenous to work patterns and because I do not use an IV strategy, these results (and those that follow) are best interpreted as descriptive and not causal. Appendix table 2 displays the results and indicates that Internet use for job search is associated with a 17.6 percentage point increase in the probability of participating, significant at the one percent level.

The preceding analysis disregards information about how long the seeker searched, but if home Internet eases transitions into participation, it may operate by allowing the individuals to become employed *sooner*. In order to incorporate all of the information available about length of time out of the labor force, I employ a duration model. I use the same method used by Kuhn and Skuterad (2004) in their analysis of Internet job search in the CPS, which addresses several unique features of the CPS sampling frame, including the fact that the CPS data is discrete, there are both left and right censored spells and eight month gaps in the data while respondents are out of the sample.[8] Table 8 displays estimates of participation hazards, which include the same control variables described above. The results indicate that, indeed, Internet job search is associated with a significant increase in hazard rates (i.e., internet search reduces non-participation durations). Thus, I conclude that Internet job search does in fact speed up transitions into participation among individuals who use Internet at home.

The evidence presented above suggests Internet job search increases the propensity to be a participant in a year's time and speeds up transitions from non-participation to participation.

---

[8]The authors develop a discrete-time hazard model that accounts for those large windows but still uses a flexible baseline hazard. See Kuhn and Skuterad (2004) for a detailed description of the model. Stata code for their paper, which was used for this paper, can be found at http://www.econ.ucsb.edu/~pjkuhn/Data/DataIndex.html.

However, there are several facts that need to be considered when gauging the magnitude of these estimated effects relative to the net effect of home Internet use on participation. The first is that a minority of individuals search for jobs online. Among non-participating married women at the time of the surveys used here (1998-2003), it was around 10 percent. According to the PEW Internet and American Life surveys, the number of women using Internet for job search has increased over time, with about 20 percent more women using Internet for job information in 2009 than 2000. However, other activities (such as reading news), experienced more than a 40 percent increase in that period.[9] If I use the estimate on participation one year later as a measure of the effect of search on participation for home Internet users, I can construct a crude "back of the envelope" estimate of the magnitude of search relative to the net effects I estimated earlier. Taking the point estimate and multiplying by the fraction of female Internet users who have used Internet for search suggests Internet job search can explain about 2.6 percentage points, or 14 percent of the estimated effects.

C.3 Home Production and Leisure

The final potential mechanisms through which home Internet usage may affect labor supply that I will consider is usage for home production and leisure. Conceptually, home production and leisure are expected to reduce/increase participation by changing the amount of time individuals spend in production of those goods (and hence, their valuation of time spent at home). To discern whether or not those mechanisms are important I consider whether there are differences between home Internet users and non-users in how much time is spent in the production of those goods. I can examine this directly using the American Time Use Survey (ATUS), a survey which records time diaries of its respondents for 24 hours periods. The survey is administered to CPS respondents, so I am able to identify home Internet users in

---

[9]Authors calculations from the PEW Internet and American Life Usage Over Time Trend Data `http://pewinternet.org/Static-Pages/Trend-Data-(Adults)/Usage-Over-Time.aspx`.

the ATUS data by linking it to the CPS Internet data.[10] I divide time use into categories: leisure, home production, and child care and I look at women age 18-59. I find that home Internet users spend 1.9 fewer hours per week in home production and 0.3 fewer hours per week in leisure. Conditional on employment, home Internet usage is associated with 1.3 fewer hours per week in home production and 0.5 more hours spent in leisure. These results, while only correlations, suggest that home Internet use is associated with a reduction in time spent in home production. The results for leisure are less clear. Interestingly, I find that home Internet users spend between 2.5-2.8 *more* hours per week in child care (depending on employment status) than non-users. This suggests some time saved in home production tasks or commuting may be used to spend time with children, and this may well be another unexplored benefit of Internet access. I leave to future work, however, to uncover whether Internet usage has a causal effect on children's well-being.

In order to gauge the relative importance of home production and leisure, I can also conduct a similar exercise to the one used in the preceding section and compare the labor force participation rates of home Internet users who use Internet for home production and leisure to home Internet users who do not. appendix table 2 displays those results, which were estimated using the same strategy outlined about for the analysis of job search. The results indicate that women who use the Internet for home production are approximately 2.5 percentage points (with a standard error of 1.7 percentage points) *more* likely to both be a participant, while those who use Internet for leisure are approximately 1.11 percentage points (with a standard error of 1.8 percentage points) *less* likely to be a participant. Neither of these results is statistically significant at conventional levels.[11] Next, I conduct a similar

---

[10]ATUS data can downloaded from ATUS-X, which also provides the procedure for linking CPS and ATUS respondents. http://www.atusdata.org/index.shtml . The ATUS is a time-use survey which asks individual to record the number of minutes spent in various activities in a 24 hour period. I convert minutes per day into hours per week. Since there can be a a large time lag between when the supplement was administered and when the ATUS is administered, I limit the sample to only those individuals who respond to the ATUS within 6 months of the CPS supplement. This leaves a sample of approximately 2000 women.

[11]Table 10 also displays participation hazards. It is not clear ex ante that use of Internet for home production should necessarily operate by reducing non-participation durations, even if it does alter the decision on whether or not to participate. Results of that analysis indicate that use of the Internet for home production has no effect on non-participation durations, while use of Internet for leisure actually increases

"back of the envelope" exercise to the one used above to scale the job search estimates. Since approximately 80 percent of women use the Internet for home production, a rough estimate like the one calculated above suggests that Internet use for home production can explain around 2 percentage points of the estimated effect, or 11 percent of the estimated increase in participation.[12] In sum, job search and home production can explain about 25 percent of the estimate effects, suggesting telework (or some other explanation) has substantial explanatory power.

---

non-participation durations.

[12]Ideally, I could compare these effects to the effect on Internet use for work to get a better sense of their relative importance of all of the mechanisms using the same framework, but unfortunately I cannot look at use of the Internet for work using this framework, since individuals in the initial survey who do not work would not report using the Internet for work in that period.

References

Ames, M. C. (2006). A review of the FCC's inside wiring rules. *Mimeo*.

Angrist, J. D. and A. B. Krueger (1992). The effect of age at school entry on educational attainment: an application of instrumental variables with moments from two samples. *Journal of the American Statistical Association 87(418)*, 328–336.

Faulhaber, G. R. (2002). Broadband deployment: Is policy in the way? In R. H. Crandall and J. H. Alleman (Eds.), *Broadband: Should We Regulate High-Speed Internet Access*, pp. 223–244. AEI-Brookings Joint Center for Regulatory Studies.

Heckman, J. J., S. Urzua, and E. Vytlacil (2006). Understanding instrumental variables in models with essential heterogeneity. *The Review of Economics and Statistics 88(3)*, 389–432.

Jackson, C. L. (2002). Wired high-speed access. In R. W. Crandall and J. H. Alleman (Eds.), *Broadband*, pp. 129–156. AEI-Brookings Joint Center for Regulatory Studies.

Kuhn, P. and H. Mansour (2011). Is internet job search still ineffective? *Working Paper*.

Kuhn, P. and M. Skuterad (2004). Internet job search and unemployment durations. *American Economic Review 94(1)*, 218–232.

Stevenson, B. (2009). The internet and job search. In D. Autor (Ed.), *Labor Market Intermediation*. University of Chicago Press.

WorldatWork (2006). WorldatWork 2006 telework trendlines; commissioned from The Dieringer Research Group Inc.

WorldatWork (2009). WorldatWork telework trendlines 2009; Data from The Dieringer Research Group Inc.

Figure 1: (Appendix) Distribution of Propensity Score P(HSI=1|X=x,Z=z)

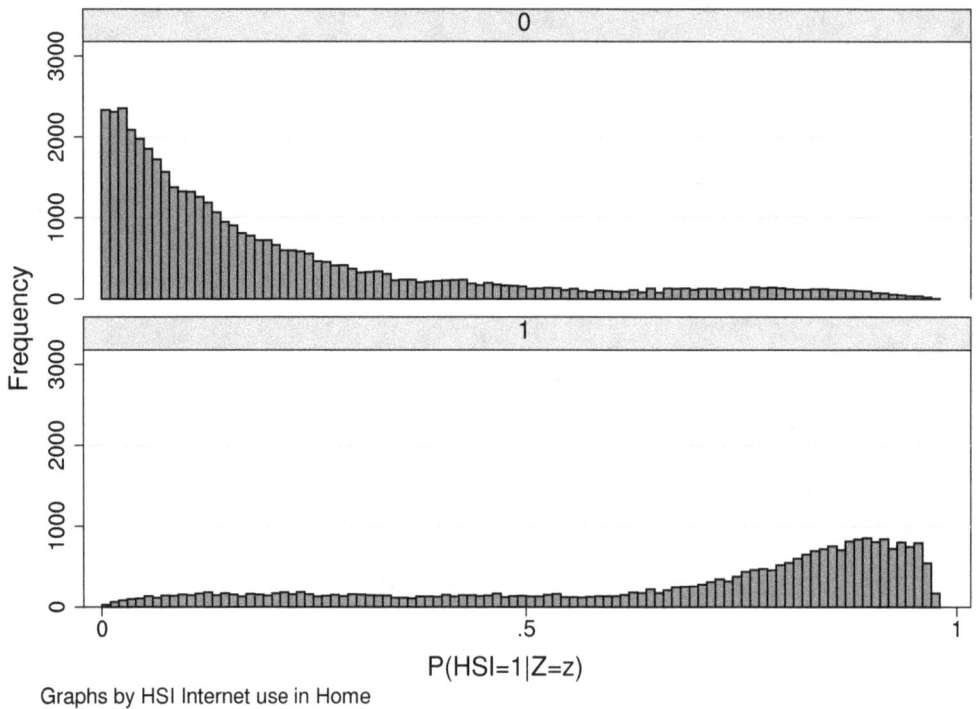

Notes: Displayed are histograms of the propensity score seperately for Internet users (HSI=1) and non-users (HSI=0). The propensity score was estimated using probit on equation (1) and calculated predicted probabilities of Internet usage.

Figure 2: (Appendix) Occupation Mean Internet Usage and Work at Home Rates

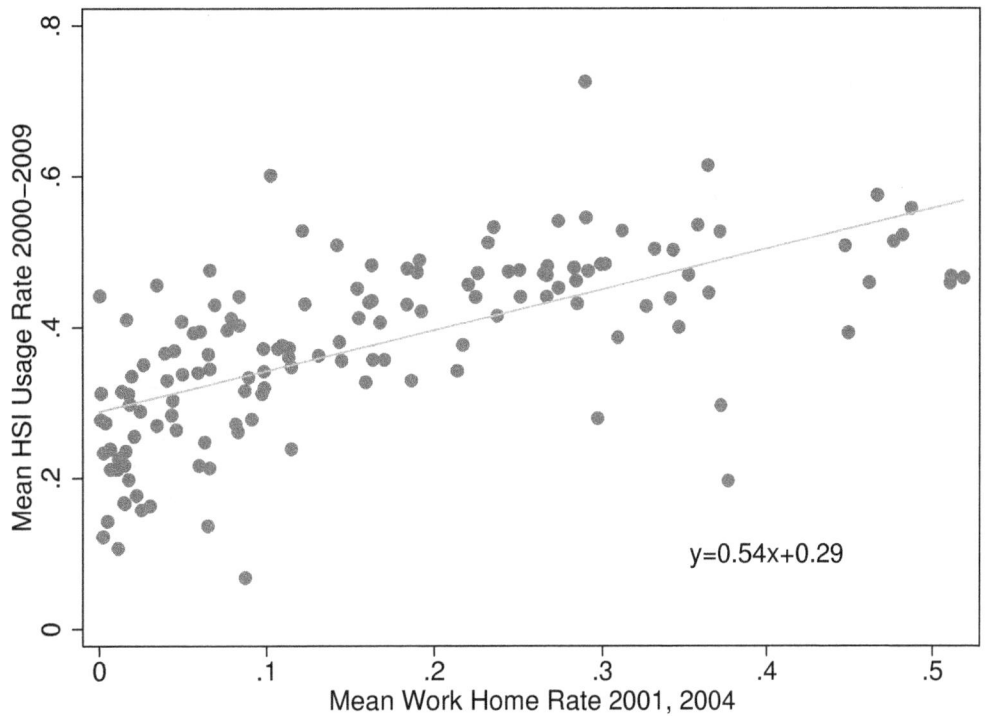

Notes: Plotted are occupation-specific work at home rates and occupation-specific high-speed Internet usage rates. Only occupations with at least 100 observations are shown and rates are calculated for working, married women 18-59. Internet usage rates were calculated in the 2000, 2001, 2003, 2007 and 2009 Current Population Survey supplements used in the main analysis and work at home rates were calculated in the 2001 and 2004 Current Population Survey work schedule supplements.

Table 1: (Appendix) Summary Statistics on Telework

	Work Home	Work Home Once Per Week+	Days Work Home	Days Home Only	Hours Worked at Home	Work Home for Family Reasons
Married Women:						
All	0.239	0.811	3.480	1.231	12.998	0.069
(N=4871)	(0.006)	(0.006)	(0.029)	(0.030)	(0.231)	(0.004)
Less than HS	0.064	0.892	4.769	3.566	32.351	0.049
(N=82)	(0.027)	(0.035)	(0.189)	(0.283)	(2.390)	(0.024)
HS/Some College	0.146	0.758	3.585	2.006	17.415	0.094
(N=1780)	(0.008)	(0.010)	(0.051)	(0.059)	(0.469)	(0.007)
College	0.436	0.841	3.388	0.756	9.886	0.056
(N=3009)	(0.009)	(0.007)	(0.035)	(0.029)	(0.219)	(0.004)
No Children	0.233	0.817	3.592	1.212	12.634	0.033
(N=2353)	(0.009)	(0.008)	(0.043)	(0.043)	(0.322)	(0.004)
Children	0.247	0.791	3.241	1.351	13.846	0.144
(N=929)	(0.014)	(0.013)	(0.064)	(0.070)	(0.559)	(0.012)
Single Women	0.164	0.763	3.282	1.010	10.861	0.045
(N=2577)	(0.007)	(0.008)	(0.040)	(0.037)	(0.282)	(0.004)
Married Men	0.228	0.812	3.268	0.898	10.954	0.043
(N=7110)	(0.005)	(0.005)	(0.025)	(0.022)	(0.170)	(0.002)

Notes: Displayed is mean and standard error of various measures of working from home. The first column includes all full time working adults 18-59. The rest of the columns include only those individuals who report working from home. N also refers to number of individuals in cell who work from home. Source: 2001 and 2004 Current Population Survey.

Table 2: (Appendix) Internet Usage and Durations of Non-Participation

	(1) LFP One year later	(2) Participation Hazard
Internet Used for Job Search	0.176***	0.454***
	(0.0219)	(0.0588)
Internet Used for Home Production	0.0248	- 0.0438
	(0.0172)	(0.0459)
Internet used for Leisure	-0.0112	- 0.0819*
	(0.0172)	(0.0460)
N	4292	4874

Notes: Column (1) displays the results for estimation of separate linear probability models for participation in the labor force 12 months after the initial survey, where the independent variable is Internet usage for the activity listed. Columns (2) displays the results estimating separate duration models as described in the text, where the dependent variable is the participation hazard for the year following the initial survey and the independent variable is Internet use for each activity. Includes controls for age, race, education, number and age of children, state of residence, and year of survey. The estimates for Internet job search also include a control for participation in active job search. The sample is limited to the married women 18-59 who use the Internet at home and were not participating in the labor force in the initial survey. Standards errors are in parentheses. * $p < .1$, ** $p < .05$, *** $p < .01$

www.ingramcontent.com/pod-product-compliance
Lightning Source LLC
Chambersburg PA
CBHW081853170526
45167CB00007B/2992